Vital Skill

Mindfulness as the Foundation of True Effectiveness

A simple approach to effective living based on being fully awake and attentive to the present moment experience

Anthony S. Jannotta

AmErica House
Baltimore

Copyright 2000 by Anthony S. Jannotta
All rights reserved. No part of this book may be reproduced in any form without written permission from the publishers, except by a reviewer who may quote brief passages in a review to be printed in a newspaper or magazine.

First printing

Those who wish to communicate with the author may reach him via e-mail by writing to him at "tony@vitalskill.com" and through the web site, "www.vitalskill.com."

ISBN: 1-58851-426-9
PUBLISHED BY AMERICA HOUSE BOOK PUBLISHERS
www.publishamerica.com
Baltimore

Printed in the United States of America

Dedication

For my wife, Jane; for my daughters, Eva and Melia; and for my son, Nolan. I love you guys more than words could ever express, and I strive each day to be mindful of your blessings.

Acknowledgments

Thanks to the following people for taking time to read the manuscript, and for their generous advice and kind words of encouragement: John Bilby, Frank Jannotta, Jane Jannotta, Melissa Mayers, Dave Meredith, and Bob Thomas. Thanks also to the folks at AmErica House.

Table of Contents

Introduction 7
    How to use this book 9
Part I 11
What is Mindfulness? 13
What is Effectiveness? 17
Where Mindfulness Meets Effectiveness 19
    The First Law of Effectiveness 23
    The Plan 24
    The Golfer 26
Present Moment Orientation 29
    Important Moments vs. Unimportant Moments 32
    Isn't it Boring? 34
    In the Moment vs. *For* the Moment 35
The Essence of Mindfulness 37
    Bare Attention 37
    The Football Guys 41
The Power of Mindfulness 45
    Quieting the Mind 45
    Labeling 46
    Non-Judgement 48
    Conscious Pausing 48
    Directness of Vision 50
Factors That Impact Your Effectiveness 51
    Beliefs 51
    Fear 54
    Worry 55
    Stress 57
    Acceptance 60
    Consequences 62
The Mindfulness Faculties of Effectiveness 65
    Clear Perception 65

　　　　Clear Recollection 66
　　　　Presence of Mind 66
　　　　The Coach 68
Part II 73
　　　　The Practice of Mindfulness 75
　　　　Objects of Mindfulness 76
　　　　Levels of Awareness 77
　　　　Approach to Practice 78
Practice Exercises 81
　　　　Conscious Breathing 81
　　　　Dedicated Practice Exercises Using the Breath 82
　　　　A Few Pointers 84
　　　　On-going Practice 89
　　　　Establishing a Daily Practice 99
　　　　Resistance 100
Part III 103
Beyond Effectiveness 105
　　　　Present Moment Goals 106
　　　　Mindfulness of Gratitude 112
　　　　Mindfulness of Love's Path 115
Conclusion 121
Appendix A: Summary of Important Points 123
Appendix B: "80 Ways" to Be More Mindful 127
Appendix C: Sources 131

Introduction

Personal effectiveness is big business. It's an industry. Individuals are hungry to feel a greater sense of happiness, success, and fulfillment in their lives. At the same time, with corporate downsizing and "re-engineering," businesses are eager to get more and more value from the time that employees spend on the job.

There are countless books, seminars, and approaches for learning to live more effectively. Most of them consist of complex systems that stress different ways of prioritizing, goal setting, organizing, and time management. I recently received a brochure for a workshop in which it was promised that the participants would master over 120 different tools—e.g. concrete steps, positive actions, foolproof principles, golden rules, essential elements, proven methods, strategies, tips, simple secrets, tried-and-true techniques, remedies, and recommendations—for becoming more effective on the job. All of this, and more, offered in a 6-hour seminar.

I do not minimize the value of these popular programs and approaches—they all have important lessons to offer. However, there is one essential, though seldom-mentioned skill, upon which all these approaches inevitably must rest, and without which all are useless. I am referring to the simple skill of *mindfulness*—the ability to be fully awake and attentive to the present moment experience.

Mindfulness is a vital skill. "Vital" is defined as follows: *of, concerned with, or manifesting life; necessary or essential to life; being a source or support of life; essential to the existence or continuation of something; of crucial importance; full of life and vigor; energetic.* "Vital" may seem like a pretty hefty word to describe something like *mindfulness*—something most people never give second thought—but I feel it is appropriate.

VITAL SKILL

This is a book about the skill of mindfulness, and how it relates to personal effectiveness. It is born of my conviction, based on my own experience and research, that mindfulness is a *vital* skill, the *ultimate* skill, and is the necessary foundation of true personal effectiveness. All meaningful skills require an investment of time and energy for their development. This book provides justification for the reader to invest in developing the skill of mindfulness.

Mindfulness, in its truest sense, is actually much more than a skill. It is listed in Buddhist doctrine as one of the "Seven Factors of Enlightenment" (the other six being *concentration, investigation of reality, energy, equanimity, tranquillity* and *rapture*). Though quiet and inconspicuous in nature, mindfulness is commonly regarded as the most fundamental of the seven factors of enlightenment, serving as the foundation for development of the rest.

The Buddha recognized the power and importance of mindfulness over 2,500 years ago, and it was the foundation of his teaching. But ultimately mindfulness has nothing to do with Buddhism, being Buddhist, or any particular philosophy or system of beliefs—it has simply to do with the art and skill of living. *Mindfulness directly addresses our ability to skillfully navigate the moments of our lives with a minimum of pain and suffering, and with as much joy, success and fulfillment as possible.* Mindfulness is as relevant to the problems, challenges, and issues of life today as it was 2500 years ago, when The Buddha was talking about it.

The purpose of this book is to make evident the practicality and importance of mindfulness for anyone wishing to be more effective in life, and to provide guidance to the reader in developing this vital skill. In Part I, we explore the meanings of mindfulness and effectiveness, and how the two are connected through The First Law of Effectiveness. We see why mindfulness is so powerful, and look at some specific manifestations of that power that are relevant to personal effectiveness. We examine various factors that affect our ability to be effective, such as beliefs, fear, worry, stress, and others, and how mindfulness impacts these factors. And we summarize by identifying the three mindfulness faculties that form the foundation of true effectiveness—clear perception, clear recollection, and presence of mind. In Part II, we look at how to go about developing mindfulness. Included is a comprehensive set of specific development techniques that can be used by anyone to begin living more mindfully, and a methodology for tailoring your practice to fit your own unique needs and preferences. And in Part III, we move *beyond* effectiveness, to what I feel are the ultimate applications of mindfulness for creating a happy, fulfilling life.

How to use this book

One of my goals in writing this book was to make it short enough that reading it from start to finish would not be such a daunting task. And that is what I recommend you do—just read it through from start to finish, and see what you think. My hope is that you will be motivated then to go back, re-read some parts, or perhaps even re-read the whole book. I believe you will find that some of the points will be more accessible the second or third time around.

I hope you will spend some extra time with Part II of the book, where I discuss the actual practice of mindfulness. I encourage you to try some of the exercises, "get your feet wet," and think about how you might be able to work some of them into your day. My ultimate goal, of course, is to demonstrate that there is enough value here for you that you eventually make mindfulness practice a part of your life. There is a wide variety of practice ideas presented here, and you should have no trouble finding a few that work well for you.

And finally, the book will be a valuable reference. It will be most useful to remind you from time to time just why it was that you took up this mindfulness practice to begin with. There will be times when you are at a loss to remember why this practice is so important; "Wait a minute. Why am I doing this anyway? What was the point of this?" It will help to flip through the book again to renew your conviction. You can also refer to Appendix A where I briefly summarize the main points of the book.

VITAL SKILL

Part I

VITAL SKILL

What is Mindfulness?

We can get a sense of what mindfulness is just by examining the word . Let's start by saying that mindfulness is the opposite of "mindlessness," or "absent-mindedness." This is accurate, and it is a good start, but "mindfulness," as it is used in this book, is much more than that. Mindfulness can be defined in many ways. To give the reader a broad understanding of what mindfulness is, I have included, in addition to my own working definition, some excerpts from other authors who address the question "What is Mindfulness?"

> "Mindfulness is a concept that is an integral part of many eastern spiritual traditions, particularly Buddhism. Simply put, it means to pay complete attention to whatever you're doing, to allow your "mind to be full" of the experience.... When you are mindful, your intention is to fully experience where you are and what you are doing..."
> (Barbara DeAngelis, from *Real Moments*, p. 6)

> "Mindfulness is the combination of concentration, clarity, and awareness brought to bear on even the smallest details of experience.... When you work with mindfulness, your movements are fluid and graceful, your thoughts clear and well organized, and your efforts effective.... You become aware of the motivation underlying your actions, and learn to catch any tendency to forget or make mistakes. As you grow skilled at being mindful, you can penetrate to a profound understanding of yourself and your actions."
> (Tarthang Tulku, from *Skillful Means*, pp. 7,8)

"Mindfulness is the process by which we go about deepening our attention and awareness, refining them, and putting them to greater practical use in our lives.... Mindfulness means paying attention in a particular way: on purpose, in the present moment, and non-judgmentally.... It is a way to take charge of the direction and quality of our own lives, including our relationships within family, our relationship to work and to the larger world and planet, and most fundamentally, our relationship with our self as a person.... Mindfulness will not conflict with any beliefs or traditions—religious or for that matter scientific—nor is it trying to sell you anything, especially not a new belief system or ideology. It is simply a practical way to be more in touch with the fullness of your being through a systematic process of self-observation, self-inquiry, and mindful action."

(Dr. Jon Kabat-Zinn, from *Wherever You Go There You Are*, pp. 4,5)

"... Thus mindfulness is at the same time a means and an end, the seed and the fruit. When we practice mindfulness in order to build up concentration, mindfulness is a seed. But mindfulness itself is the life of awareness: the presence of mindfulness means the presence of life, and therefore mindfulness is also the fruit. Mindfulness frees us of forgetfulness and dispersion [of mind] and makes it possible to live fully each minute of life. Mindfulness enables us to live."

(Thich Nhat Hanh, from *The Miracle of Mindfulness*, p. 15)

A skill, a discipline, a practice, a process, a way of life, a way of being—mindfulness is all of these things. For our purposes I define mindfulness as follows: **Mindfulness is the skill of being fully awake and attentive to the present moment experience, with open acceptance of whatever is there.** Using this definition, there are three main points:

1. We will view mindfulness as a skill. The development of any skill requires three components: *conviction, commitment*, and *practice*.

   Conviction is present when you become *convinced* that a skill is worth the investment of time and effort that would be necessary to develop it.

   Commitment is present when you *commit* yourself to doing whatever it takes to develop the particular skill. The development of the skill becomes a top priority.

   Practice is the component that leads to the actual development of the skill. Whether it is swimming, golf, playing the piano, or mindfulness, *practice* is the one and only way that a skill can be developed. It makes no difference how many books you read, how many lessons you take, or how much time you spend thinking about developing a particular skill; if you do not *practice*, you will never actually develop and become proficient at it. *Conviction* and *commitment* must be present before practice will take place.

2. Mindfulness means paying attention, on a consistent and sustained basis, to the present moment experience. This involves anchoring your attention, awareness and consciousness in the present moment. It means being awake and attentive to what you are doing and what is happening, both within and outside yourself, right here, right now.

3. Mindfulness requires openly accepting whatever exists in the present moment. At times it is difficult and painful to accept the situations that life presents. With mindfulness, you come to recognize what conditions, expectations and judgements you impose upon the present moment that may add to the difficulty of accepting the present moment as it is:

    —What conditions have you placed on the present moment that must be met before you will allow yourself to feel satisfied and content?

VITAL SKILL

—What expectations do you have, perhaps regarding the results of your efforts or the outcome of a particular situation, which may be a source of anxiety or disappointment?
—What judgements—good or bad, right or wrong—do you place upon yourself, your situation, or the people and things around you, that make it impossible to feel at peace and to openly accept what exists in the present moment?

Of course, some level of mindfulness is present in all of us. After all, if we were completely *unable* to attend to the present moment experience, how would we manage to get up in the morning, get to work, or get food on the table? The only reason to further develop the skill of mindfulness is so that we can live life *more* mindfully. Living life mindfully, in my own experience, is characterized by a heightened sense of wakefulness, clarity, calm and stability. In the context of mindfulness, I define these terms as follows:

—Wakefulness—the sense of being very alert to what is happening in the moment, even the more subtle aspects of the present moment experience. This includes awareness of internal thoughts and feelings as well as external situations and events.
—Clarity—your thoughts, feelings, and perceptions are clear, distinct, and recognizable—they are not clouded by beliefs or fear.
—Calm—you accept things as they are. You are not easily excited or agitated by external events, or by your own beliefs, fears, judgements, expectations, emotions, thoughts, and feelings.
—Stability—the sense of having a solid base, or foundation. You know exactly where you are, what you are doing, what is going on inside you—body and mind, and what is happening around you.

What is Effectiveness?

The concept of effectiveness can be applied to every aspect of our lives. Personal relationships, business, career, parenthood, managing stress, spirituality and learning to play golf are just some of the areas where effectiveness is relevant. There really is no area of life where effectiveness is not required—where we don't, at some point, want to affect some change, or create a particular result.

Let's begin by defining effectiveness in the simplest way possible: *Effectiveness is the ability to produce a definite and desired result.* We can take this definition a step further by introducing the concept of "true effectiveness": *True Effectiveness is the ability to produce a definite and desired result, which contributes to your experience of success and fulfillment in life.*

We have all had the experience of working hard to produce a particular result, only to feel disappointed and unfulfilled when we finally succeed. Though we successfully produced the desired result, it didn't end up making us feel the way we hoped. In a situation like this we have been "effective," but haven't been "*truly* effective." *True effectiveness* is what we are really after, so I adopt this definition as our general definition for "effectiveness."

We will incorporate the broadest possible interpretation of the above definition. As it is used here, "result" does not simply mean "output" or "production". The result you wish to produce may be specific and tangible; e.g. "lose 10 pounds by New Years," or more broad and intangible; e.g. "be happier and more joyful at work and at home." Your desired result could be to complete a specific task, to create a more intimate relationship with your spouse, to reduce your stress level, to manage anger more effectively, to heal a physical ailment, or to make more money. In this sense, effectiveness has nothing to do, necessarily, with productivity, busyness, or simply "getting the job done." Likewise, we use the word "success" not as society would define it, but rather as our *hearts* define it. True success for you may mean something completely different from what it would mean for me. *True fulfillment and success are entirely a function of your individual life purpose and heart's desire.*

Where Mindfulness Meets Effectiveness

To demonstrate how mindfulness and effectiveness are linked, we must analyze what actually happens when a person successfully produces a "definite and desired result." For this I use a graphical representation of time, beginning with a time line. (Fig. 1)

Time

Past   Future

Figure 1

The time line in Figure 1 is made up of dashes. If we take a "close-up" view of it (Fig. 2), we see that each dash represents a *moment*.

Time

⟵   ⟵   ⟵   ⟵   ⟵
Moment   Moment   Moment   Moment   Moment   Moment   Moment

Past   Future

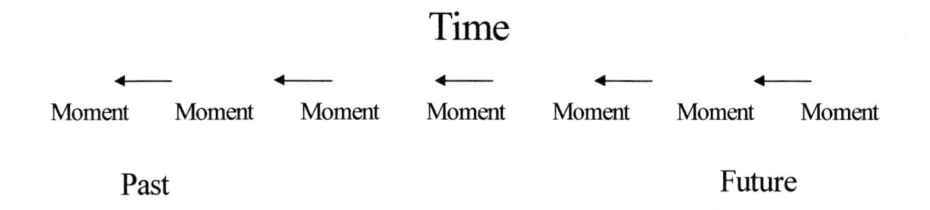

Figure 2

VITAL SKILL

For this discussion, we consider time to consist of an endless succession of moments. To simulate the passage of time, we can imagine these moments are *"moving"* from right to left in the figure (see arrows), i.e. from the future (right), into the past (left). (Of course, in reality, time is not made up of individual moments that "move." This is simply a model, or image, used to graphically illustrate the passage of time.)

In Figure 3 we define the "Present Moment Position" on the time line (indicated in the middle), which is "stationary" in the figure. Again, to represent the passage of time we imagine the time line (the endless succession of moments) to be "moving" from right to left. That is, a "future moment" eventually becomes the "present moment", and then becomes a "past moment." In our figure, the time line "moves" while the present moment remains stationary. "Real world events" are shown occurring in the present moment, and only in the present moment.

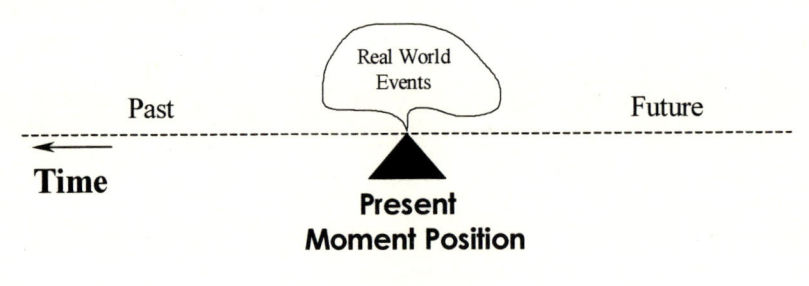

Figure 3

Example
Fig. 4 shows a random stretch of time on the time line, with two moments indicated—moments "a" and "z." Moment "z" is in the future relative to moment "a." For our example we will designate moment "a" as the moment some particular "desired result" is

conceived, and moment "z" as the moment, some time later, that particular result is *achieved*.

Result Conceived   **Result Achieved**

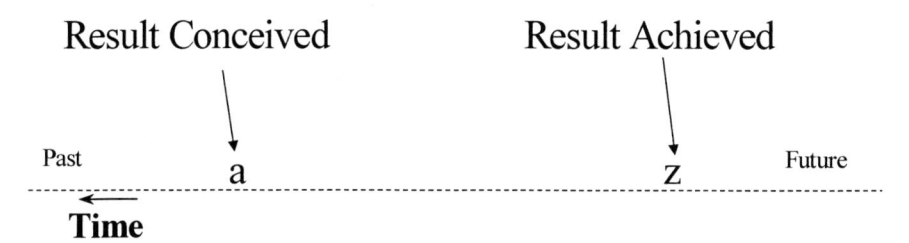

Past ——————— a ——————————————— z ——————— Future
← Time

Figure 4

Let's pretend that you, the reader, conceived of this desired result you wanted to produce, at moment "a," and deliberately set out to achieve it, eventually succeeding at moment "z."

There is a time lapse between the moment a desired result is conceived, and the moment that result is achieved. In our example, that time lapse consists of the successive moments that occur between moments "a" and "z," which we will designate as moments "b-y." (Fig. 5)

Result Conceived   **Result Achieved**

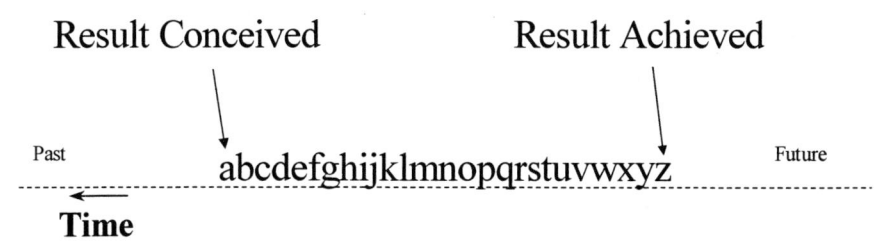

Past ——— abcdefghijklmnopqrstuvwxyz ——— Future
← Time

Figure 5

If you claim to have been *effective* in producing this desired result (conceived at moment "a" and achieved at moment "z"), it would have to be as a result of your influence upon events taking place during moments "b-y." In other words, it would be your *efforts*, your

VITAL SKILL

performance, your *ability to make certain things happen* during the moments "b-y," that end in the desired result being achieved at moment "z." The better, more competent your performance during moments "b-y," the more effective you would be.

Now, let's take a closer look at the real world events in this example. If we "step out" of time and examine the moments "b-y," observing moment-by-moment the events, as they happen, two things are certain:

1. The events that take place in moments "b-y," and your influence upon them, do not happen all at once, but happen *one moment at a time*. That is, the events of moment "b" take place after moment "a" is finished, then the events of moment "c" happen, then the events of moment "d," then moment "e," and so on, through to moment "y," and finally moment "z" when the desired result is achieved. (Fig. 5)

2. The events of each individual moment, "b-y," and your influence upon them, happen when, and only when, that particular moment is the *present moment*. For example, the events of moment "m" happen only when moment "m" is the present moment (i.e. in the "present moment position" on our illustration—see Fig. 6).

Result Conceived   Result Achieved

Past   abcdefghijklmnopqrstuvwxyz   Future

Time

Present Moment Position

(events of moment "m" happening "now")

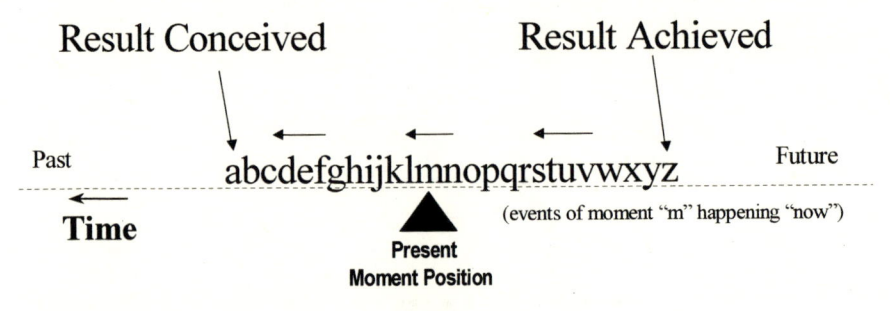

Figure 6

Summarizing our example:

—We noted that effectiveness is a result of your influence upon the events occurring in moments "b-y."

—We also noted, with the two observations above, that the events of moments "b-y" happen *one moment at a time,* and happen *only in the present moment.*

Combining these two points, we must conclude that *effectiveness itself* happens *one moment at a time, in the present moment.*

The First Law of Effectiveness

This is a crucial principle that applies not only to our example, but to effectiveness in general. Personal effectiveness, in any situation, can only happen *one moment at a time, in the present moment.* This point is so important that I establish it as ***The First Law of Effectiveness***, which states:

***Effectiveness happens one moment at a time,
in the present moment.***

The present moment is where mindfulness and effectiveness unite. To be effective in life, you must be effective one moment at a time, in the present moment. Being effective in the present moment requires mindfulness!

VITAL SKILL

Mindfulness & Effectiveness

Past — Time — Present Moment — Future

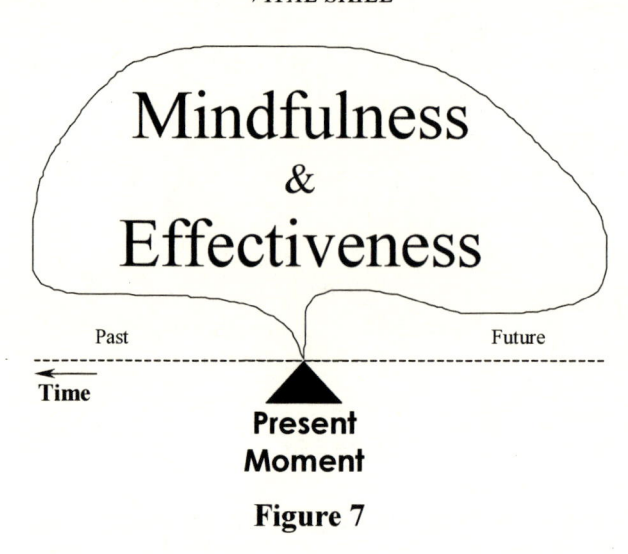

Figure 7

Marsha Sinetar is a psychologist, mediator, and author, who writes:

"Mindfulness puts us in a constant present [moment], releasing us from the clatter of distracting thoughts so that our energy, creativity, and productivity are undiluted. [With mindfulness] you become your most effective. Attention is power, and those who work in a state of mindful awareness bring an almost supernatural power to what they do." (from *Mindfulness and Meaningful Work*, p. 221)

The Plan

Perhaps you have read books, or attended seminars, that focused on planning and goal setting as the keys to effectiveness. If so, you have probably clarified your life priorities, examined the relationship between your life priorities and work priorities, looked at constructive lifestyle changes that are more in line with your priorities, developed a more effective time management system, and established attainable short, medium, and long term goals. At the end of it all, you may have come up with a detailed plan to follow, clearly written out, incorporating all that you had learned, and designed to help you reach the goals you established.

At this point you would have invested a fair amount of your time, energy, and perhaps money, with the end result being this "plan." I am not knocking planning—there is no doubt that planning is essential for accomplishing your goals—but we should recognize that a plan is of limited value. Your plan, by itself, is nothing more than a sheet of paper with a bunch of words written on it. It is the *execution* of your plan that really counts. If you never execute your plan, you may as well not have a plan. Even if you have the most brilliant plan ever conceived, it is only as good as your *execution* of it.

The insight you gained in that seminar concerning your life priorities; the concepts and methods of goal-setting, organizing, and time management you learned; and the goals and plan of action that you laid out, are relevant *only* as they are consciously applied in the present moment. Action can only be taken *one moment at a time, in the present moment*. This means that the execution of your plan can only happen *one moment at a time, in the present moment*.

Executing a meaningful plan often requires confronting fears, beliefs, habits, perceived risks, etc., which would stand in the way of your taking the actions that must be taken. This is where most plans fall apart. Effective execution of a plan requires the ability to work through these obstructing fears, beliefs, habits, and perceived risks. You must also be able to clearly see when your plan needs to be revised or even abandoned. We will see how mindfulness practice, by strengthening your ability to be conscious and aware in the present moment, can help you effectively execute your plan.

Having clearly stated plans and goals gives you a sense of having taken control of your future, but this is pure illusion. The "future" is really nothing more that an idea or concept. The only thing we know for certain about the future is that it really doesn't exist until it actually occurs, *in the present moment*. The future *manifests*—becomes *real*—only in the present moment. In fact, *the present moment is your future—they are one and the same*. The one and only way you can achieve any sense of control over your future is to gain a sense of control over your present moment experience. This requires mindfulness.

The Golfer

Of course, everyone employs some level of mindfulness, and therefore some level of effectiveness. We could not survive otherwise, but it is a matter of degree. Using a golf analogy, almost anyone could get through a round of golf if they had to. For some non-golfers it could take days, and would not be too enjoyable. But most people who want to play golf find it worthwhile to take some lessons and spend time practicing, in an effort to improve their game, with the expectation that this will make the game more enjoyable.

With respect to mindfulness, the questions is this: *Is it worthwhile to undertake a deliberate effort to increase our level of mindfulness, as a way of increasing our effectiveness, and thus our experience of success and fulfillment in life?* Most of us would probably answer: "Well, that depends. Would it really make that much difference?" Indeed it would.

Returning to the golf analogy, a beginning golfer could most likely complete a round of golf, given enough time. Let's suppose it took him several days. If he had never before been exposed to the game—knew nothing about golf—he might go away from that first round feeling he was a pretty good golfer. It may not be until he watched a golf tournament on television that he would see what a high level of skill is possible in the game, and how much room he has for improvement. If he then undertook to learn and practice the game, with proper guidance, there is an enormous amount of improvement he would make after a year or so of consistent effort. The round of golf he would play after that year of practice and instruction would be immeasurably better than his first round.

The point is: *As much improvement as there is to be made in the game of golf for the beginner, there is a comparable amount of improvement that can be realized by most of us in the area of mindfulness, and thus effectiveness.* Most of us are not aware of this because we don't recognize the effects of mindfulness when we see them, so we don't know what is possible; we have no frame of reference. Unlike the game of golf, there are no mindfulness tournaments on television where we can see high levels of mindfulness demonstrated.

But anytime we see someone perform with excellence, whether it is in sports, the arts, politics, business, or wherever; we are seeing, among other things, the effects of *focused and sustained attention* upon the task at hand. The single most critical element for excellence in doing anything is *focused and sustained attention*. Mindfulness is simply the practice and skill of applying focused and sustained attention upon the experience of everyday life. It means living life with your attention and awareness in the present moment. To increase your effectiveness—your ability to perform with excellence all the time, in all aspects of life—the essential first step is the development of mindfulness.

A good example is professional basketball great Michael Jordan. In January 1999, when Michael Jordan announced his retirement from the Chicago Bulls, and professional basketball, I heard a Chicago based sports writer on radio who had followed Jordan's career closely. He was discussing the attributes that made Jordan so great. The non-physical attribute that the sports writer felt was the biggest contributor to Jordan's greatness was his ability to be *completely in the present moment during the game*. The writer felt this was the reason Jordan performed so well and so consistently under such immense pressure. Jordan himself addresses this topic in his book *For the Love of the Game*. Discussing his extraordinary ability he writes:

> "Where did it come from? I don't know. That's like asking an artist where his inspiration comes from. Phil Jackson told us many times to deal with what's happening right now. It's an idea that always has been with me. My heart and my soul are in the moment. The best thing about living that way is that you don't know what the next moment is going to bring. And that

VITAL SKILL

was the best thing about the way I played the game. No one, not even me, knew what I was going to do next. If I had to pick one characteristic about my game, that would be it. I always thought I performed my best when I didn't know what was coming.... Tomorrow I don't know what I'm going to do. I think about today. People can't believe I don't know what's going to happen next week, next month, next year. But I truly live in the moment." (from Michael Jordan, *For the Love of the Game*)

Present Moment Orientation

The First Law of Effectiveness can be generalized to arrive at the First Law of Life, which states: *Life happens one moment at a time, in the present moment.* I call this perspective a *Present Moment Orientation.*

LIFE

ALL THAT HAPPENS. ALL THAT IS.

Past   Future

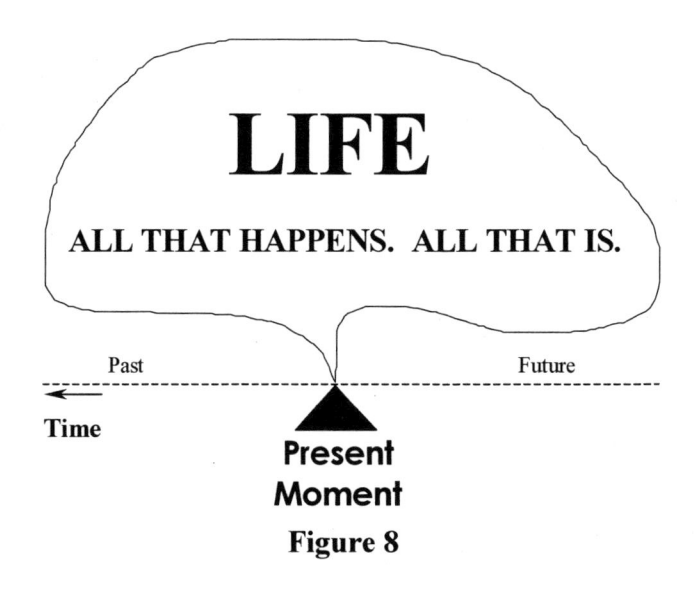

Time   **Present Moment**

Figure 8

Figure 8 conveys the essence of a present moment orientation, which basically involves conscious awareness of the fact that; "life, all that happens, all that is," all experience, absolutely everything, is completely contained within the present moment. Life happens only in the present moment. The past is gone and the future has not yet happened—the only thing that is real is what is here and now.

VITAL SKILL

Your very life consists solely of the events that happen, one moment at a time, here and now, in the present moment. You cannot be effective if you are "thinking about other things" while the present moment (<u>your</u> <u>life</u>) is taking place.

The present moment experience is the very *substance* of your life—there is nothing else. You have a past and a future, but past and future are merely *ideas*, or *concepts* that exist only when you are *thinking* about them in the present moment. Your past and future give rise to what we could call your *"life situation,"* but we must distinguish between your "life situation," and your "life." Your "life situation" is the circumstance, or situation in which you find yourself. It consists of your occupation, relationships, past experience, financial status, and all else that is external to you. But your *"life"* is independent of your past, future, or anything external. Your "life" consists of nothing other than your actual present moment experience.

Without mindfulness, you miss out on your "life," and you lose all sense of control over your "life situation." You miss what life has to offer you, and you miss your only chance to be effective. This is why mindfulness is such a *vital* skill. In his book, *The Practice of Happiness*, psychologist Mirko Fryba makes this point in the first chapter, entitled "Mindful Mastery of Life," which begins:

"This very situation you are experiencing here and now, dear reader, is the most real reality of your life. Only here and now can you accomplish something, undertake something, to structure your life so that things will go the way you want them to in the future. The future is not yet real, and the past is no longer real enough for you to be able to do anything to change it. Only by paying attention to the possibilities that exist for you here and now will you master your life."

(Mirko Fryba, from *The Practice of Happiness*, p. 1)

The Shower

The notion that your entire life consists solely of the events of the present moment may be hard to accept. Consider the example of taking a shower—a fairly routine, mundane event for most of us. During a shower, your life consists solely of the experience of taking that shower—e.g. the feeling of the warm water hitting your skin, the washcloth scrubbing your skin, the steamy air, and whatever thoughts and feelings you might have in those moments. And that's it. During the moments of that shower, the experiences, or the events that happen in that shower are *everything*, and they deserve your complete attention.

You may be thinking: "Give me a break. I have a career, a marriage, three kids (the oldest of which needs braces), a house that needs work, I'm trying to keep healthy, I have hobbies and things I like doing, and on and on. This particular shower is one of about a *million* showers I will take in my lifetime. It's not *'everything'*—it's just *another shower!'* This is an understandable viewpoint—even while you are in that shower, it seems there are so many more important and more interesting things in your life than what is going on in that shower.

But suppose that during that shower, while you are scrubbing your back and singing a song, or thinking about the important meetings you have scheduled that day, you step on a bar of soap, slip, fall, and break your leg. Suddenly there you are, sitting in the shower with a broken leg, unable to get up.

For the first few moments after this happens, your meetings, family, career, house, hobbies, etc., all seem to vanish, and your attention is focused entirely on the experience of the moment (namely, the experience of sitting in the shower with a broken leg). In those moments, there truly is *nothing* more deserving of your attention than what is happening right then and there—you're stuck, helpless, and in great pain. Of course, within a short time, thoughts of all the ramifications of your situation will fill your mind. All kinds of changes, arrangements, and adjustments will be necessary to accommodate your newly broken leg. In fact no part of your life would be unaffected by the event that just happened, in that "routine, mundane" shower.

Now, granted, this is an unusual situation. But I would make the point that there really is nothing special or magical about a "crisis" like breaking your leg in the shower—it's just an event, or an experience, like the experience of feeling warm water hitting your skin. In reality it is no more deserving of your attention than any other event or experience. But at the same time, a momentary, unexpected "crisis" like this has the potential of completely and irrevocably changing your life, and it forces you to recognize and deal with the one and only true reality of your life—*that which is happening here and now, in the present moment.* It helps you appreciate the fact that each and every moment really *does* count—each moment has the potential of completely and irrevocably changing your life. A crisis makes unavoidable the fact that the present moment experience really is all there is.

It is worth noting that many of the "crises" we are familiar with (e.g. almost any kind of accident) result directly from not paying attention to the present moment experience. Fortunately, you do not require a crisis to live in the present moment—you can begin right now. It is worthwhile to strive to live mindfully, with your awareness and attention anchored in the present moment.

Important Moments vs. Unimportant Moments

"O.K. But as long as I am careful not to break my leg, so what if I daydream, or think about work while showering, or washing dishes? What does that have to do with my ability to be effective while in a meeting with a client, or when dealing with my children?" Fair enough. It's a good point. In fact there is no *direct* connection between, say, what you think about in the shower and your ability to be effective in a business meeting. But there is, at the very least, an *indirect* connection.

It is tempting to think of some moments as being "important", and other moments as "unimportant". "Important" moments are those moments in which something we consider important is happening. "Unimportant" moments are those moments where nothing of much importance is happening.

It makes sense that being mindful during the "important" moments is a good idea—this is when something *important* is happening and we want to be fully present and aware in order to perform our very best, or to get the most out of the experience. At the same time, it may not seem so critical to be mindful during the "unimportant" moments, like in the shower, when nothing *important* is happening—where our best performance is not required, or the experience at hand is not considered particularly special. So you wonder: "Why not just be mindful during the 'important' moments, and not worry about it the rest of the time? *What's the big deal?"*

You will find that if you have not practiced to develop mindfulness during the "unimportant" moments, you simply cannot count on being mindful during the "important" moments. During those "important" moments, like in a business meeting, you most likely will not be thinking about mindfulness. You may be generally aware of whatever is going on, but your mind will be largely distracted by all the thoughts, feelings, fears, daydreams, fantasies, etc., that arise therefrom. Practicing mindfulness in those "unimportant" moments develops the tendency to be mindful. It develops the *energy* that awakens you from distraction so that you can return to the present moment experience. This can only be developed through practice.

Take a professional musician. You might consider the most "important" moments for a professional musician to be the moments he is on stage performing, and other moments to be relatively "unimportant" as far as his music career is concerned. After all, it is only when he performs on stage that he gets to showcase his art. And, no less important, that is where he makes his money to live on. But we all know that for every moment a talented professional musician spends on stage, there have been countless moments spent off somewhere alone, practicing technique and musical expression, and learning new material. The professional musician knows there is no way he could be effective during those "important" moments on stage unless he had committed a lot of his off-stage, "unimportant" moments to practicing.

More relevant to our everyday life, "important" moments do not typically give advance warning that they are coming. They don't reach out and tap you on the shoulder, announcing their arrival, so that you can begin paying attention. They usually come and go quietly, without fanfare. If you are not mindful during the "unimportant" moments, you will no doubt miss many of the "important" ones as well. Therefore, if you want to be mindful in the "important" moments, as we all do, you need to practice and develop mindfulness in the "unimportant" moments. Part II of the book covers how this can be done. For the purpose of developing mindfulness, the so-called "unimportant" moments are actually very important.

Isn't it Boring?

"But it sounds so boring, just paying attention to what is happening in the moment." It may seem that way when you first start thinking about it, but the opposite is true. If being mindful sounds boring, or unexciting, the real question is this: *What are all the exciting things you are afraid you would miss while paying attention to the present moment experience?* There is nothing there to miss. Since nothing happens but in the present moment, you won't miss a thing. In fact you'll be more present to whatever actually does happen.

You may be concerned about missing out on all the little fantasies and daydreams that are your constant companions, and *seem* to add excitement to your life. But you need not worry about that—the fantasies and daydreams will still be there, as always. The only difference is that by developing mindfulness, you will begin seeing them more and more clearly. You will hang on to your fantasies and daydreams until mindfulness ultimately reveals them to you as they actually are—empty, boring, and without value. Only after their true nature is fully recognized will you begin to let go of your fantasies and daydreams.

In the Moment vs. *For* the Moment

With a present moment orientation, living in the present moment simply makes sense. But it is helpful to distinguish between living *in* the present, and living *for* the present.

Living *for* the present suggests living for instant, present moment gratification or pleasure, without any concern for the future. Working toward long term goals and purposes is not consistent with living *for* the present moment. On the other hand, living *in* the present, a primary aspect of mindfulness, simply means living with your attention, awareness, and consciousness focused on the present moment experience. Mindfulness does not preclude thinking, planning, and preparing for the future.

Suppose you had the habit of meticulously planning and plotting every aspect of your life, and deferring all gratification and pleasure until after all your goals have been achieved. Living this way, deferring gratification and pleasure to the future, you could not be said to be living *for* the present, but there would certainly be no conflict with living mindfully, *in* the present. After all, planning and plotting can only happen in the present moment, and there is no reason you can't do that *in* the moment, with your attention, awareness, and consciousness focused on the present moment experience. And if you were to most effectively execute your plan, it would be critical for you to live *in* the present, with mindfulness, because the execution of that plan can only happen one moment at a time, in the present moment. In a case like this, however, the chief benefit of mindfulness may be that you would begin to see the absurdity of excessive planning, plotting, and deferment of gratification. Mindfulness, in this case, may help you learn to stop and "smell the roses" along the way.

Living *in* the present moment does not mean we can never think about the past or future. It can be very useful to think about the past or future. Reflection upon past events can give us valuable insight and understanding, and some planning for the future is essential. Mindfulness simply ensures that, when we think about the past or future, we are conscious and in control. It means our thinking is not able to "run away with us", escaping our conscious control and taking us down endless paths of unhelpful thoughts. A present moment orientation is very practical and sensible, and is essential for realizing true effectiveness.

The Essence of Mindfulness

The essence, the "building block," and the fundamental source of power of mindfulness, is *Bare Attention*.

Bare Attention

The practice and development of mindfulness is very simple—all we really do is *observe*. We simply practice *paying attention*. Mindfulness is developed by the systematic and deliberate application of "*bare attention*" to our present moment experience. The "practice of mindfulness" basically boils down to the practice of *bare attention*. Buddhist scholar Nyanaponika Thera defines bare attention as follows:

> "By bare attention we understand the clear and single-minded awareness of what actually happens *to* us and *in* us, at the successive moments of perception. It is called "bare" because it attends to the bare facts of a perception without reacting to them by deed, speech, or mental comment." (Nyanaponika Thera, from *The Power of Mindfulness*, p. 5)

In practicing bare attention we cultivate the discipline of sustained, moment-to-moment attention to our present moment experience, without judgement, analysis, or concern for results or benefits.

The first key phrase here is "sustained, moment-to-moment attention to our present moment experience." This means paying attention over a sustained period of time, attending to *each successive moment*; i.e. moment-to-moment. This quality of attention to present moment experience is *foreign* to most of us.

Let's return to our time-line model, with a random stretch of time, moments "a-z." Our ordinary existence can be illustrated, somewhat simplistically, as shown in Figure 9.

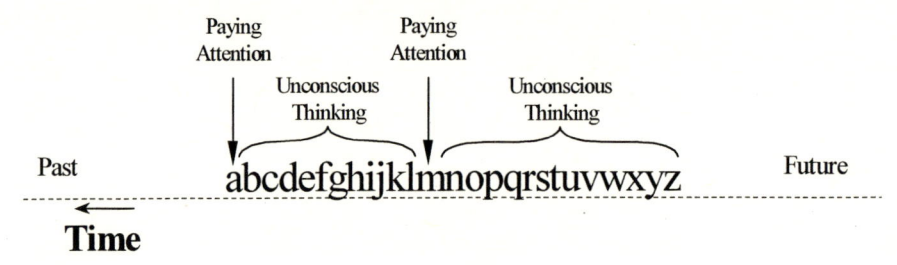

Figure 9

In our normal state of consciousness, most moments are consumed with unconscious thought. We pay attention to the present moment experience for a moment here or there (like moments "a" and "m," indicated with arrows in Fig. 10), but most of the time we are wrapped up in unconscious thought processes that last for many moments in a row (like moments "b-l" and "n-z"). This pattern is so ingrained, and has become so natural to us, that it goes entirely unnoticed and unquestioned. This unconscious thinking may be related to something we have observed in a moment of attention—e.g. we momentarily observe our experience, then automatically fall into a chain of reactive thoughts, feelings, judgements, analysis—or it may be related to nothing in particular. The point is, during these periods of thought we miss what is actually happening—we are *absent and unavailable* to what we are doing, and what is going on in and around us in the present moment.

Thinking itself is not the problem—focused, purposeful thinking is an essential and powerful tool. The purpose of mindfulness is *not* to stop thinking. The problem is that the thinking pattern described above is entirely unconscious and uncontrolled—it is neither focused nor purposeful. As we begin working with bare attention, we find *we are not aware of our own minds!* We see how little of the time we are actually awake and attentive to the present moment reality. And we see how predominant, and utterly *devoid of value,* our unconscious thinking activity really is—it is mostly a confused jumble of worry, regret, anxiety, fantasy, daydreaming, judgment, craving, rehashing past events, rehearsing future events, etc.—what I refer to as *"mental noise." We gain nothing of value from mental noise!*

Exercise: You can get a sense of this by doing the following simple exercise:
1. Turn to page 82 and review practice exercise # 1, "Counting the Breath."
2. Sit down with a pencil, paper, and a timer.
3. Practice the "counting your breath" exercise for a period of 5—10 minutes.
4. Doing the exercise you will notice a tendency to become distracted and lose count. Each time you notice this (i.e. when you awaken from the distraction) make a hash mark on the paper. Then return directly to the exercise, beginning again at "1."
5. Each time you manage to maintain the count for 10 straight breaths, and return to "1," make a check mark on the paper, and continue.

When finished, examine what you have written. If there are few or no check marks, do not be discouraged—for the majority of people trying it the first time, this will be the case.

Try the exercise again. This time, when you notice your mind has wandered, try to recall and note the general nature of the thoughts you were having just before awakening—e.g. "worrying," "daydreaming," "fantasizing," "regretting," "rehashing," "rehearsing," "planning." If it is difficult to find the right label, just use "daydreaming."

Take some time to ponder what you experienced doing this exercise.

VITAL SKILL

Did you experience this exercise as difficult, or unpleasant?
Were you able to concentrate for this short period of time?
What was the highest count you reached?
Were your thoughts clear and distinct enough that you could recall and label them?
What sorts of thoughts were seizing your attention?

In contrast to Figure 9, Figure 10 illustrates bare attention. Practicing bare attention, we are attentive to the present moment experience, moment-to-moment, on a sustained, continuing basis. The quality of attention we cultivate with this practice is focused and concentrated. It has the strength to resist distraction. It is this sustained, focused attention that makes mindfulness so powerful. *Everything we need know, every secret of life, is right here in front of us. All we really need to do is pay attention.*

Bare Attention

Past　　　abcdefghijklmnopqrstuvwxyz　　　Future

Time

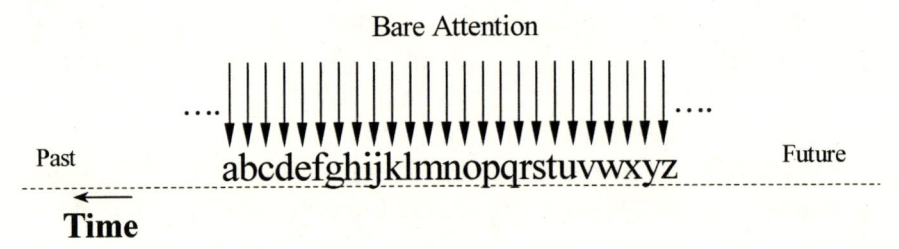

Figure 10

Figure 10 also illustrates the second key phrase pertaining to bare attention: "without judgement, analysis, or concern for results or benefits." In practicing bare attention we are not trying to figure things out, find answers to questions, determine whether something is good or bad, or change anything. Notice that there are no moments devoted to thinking in Figure 10. "Judgement, analysis, or concern for results or benefits" amount to nothing more than "thinking." It is not possible to practice bare attention, *while* thinking, all at the same time. Generally speaking, if we are paying attention, we are not thinking; and if we are thinking, we are not paying attention. In the practice of bare attention, the emphasis is on *paying attention*. Any beneficial analysis or consideration of what is happening will occur on its own, so it need not be part of the practice. The real power of practicing bare attention lies in *repetition*—witnessing *over and over and over again* our actions, responses, thoughts, feelings, etc., as they occur, in the present moment. Understanding and insight are the inevitable result.

You need not concern yourself with what might happen if you become so mindful that you stop thinking all together—that would be next to impossible. Thinking is inevitable and spontaneous. There is no way that thinking will not occur. Just as you could not survive without some measure of mindfulness, you could not survive without your capacity to think. Likewise, bare attention will never get in your way when you *need* to think. If you have a busy, hectic job, with 1,000 things going on at once, it may seem impossible to practice bare attention as we are describing it here, while at work. Fortunately, this is not a problem. In Part II we discuss ways that even the busiest of us can incorporate mindfulness practice into our day.

It deserves repeating that *thinking* itself is not a problem, and it is not a bad thing. It is the random, unconscious, and uncontrolled thinking (mental noise) which contributes nothing to your effectiveness that needs to be brought under control.

The Football Guys

Consider two friends who get together every Sunday during football season to watch football games on TV. Suppose they each have different levels of interest in football. One is only *mildly* interested in the game. During the game, he is in and out of the room, watching only a play or two at a time. Most of the time he is either talking on the phone, cooking, reading the paper, or some other such thing. He may see an average of only four or five plays per quarter of any given game. We can call him "The Glancer" since he only *glances* at the game now and then. The other guy is just the opposite. He is *very* interested in the game. He watches every play of the entire game, from start to finish, very attentively. We can call him "The Watcher" since he truly *watches* the games.

With any particular game, The Glancer, though he does not actually see much of the game, still ends up knowing quite a lot about it. He knows which teams played, where they played, who the starting and finishing players were, the general progression of scoring during the game, who won, and there are other things about the game he would know as well. If someone asked him on Monday, whether he saw the game, he could fairly answer that he did see the game, and could probably hold his own in a conversation about it.

The Watcher, on the other hand, having watched the whole game with attention, would know *far more* about the game than The Glancer. The Watcher would know, in detail, the key plays, key players, important penalties, player substitutions, turnovers, errors, coaching decisions and strategies. He would know who won the game, and would have an informed opinion as to why they won. If The Glancer and The Watcher were to have a conversation about the game, it would be evident that The Glancer actually knew *very little* about that particular game compared to The Watcher.

To take it a step further, imagine that this went on every week for the entire season—these two got together every Sunday and watched football as described above. By the end of the season, The Watcher would not only know much more than The Glancer about each specific game they had seen, but he would also have *vastly* more knowledge and understanding of the game of football itself. He would have a much more intimate appreciation of each team, the players, the coaches, the rules of the game, the different stadiums, the general tactics of winning, and many of the subtleties and finer points of football. In fact, by the end of the season, The Watcher would be a football *expert* compared to The Glancer. And there is nothing surprising or mysterious about this; it's only because The Watcher was *paying attention to the games*, while The Glancer was not. If you were to choose which of these two would make a more effective football coach, you would have to go with The Watcher!

VITAL SKILL

The "Football Guys" example becomes relevant if we compare the game of football to the "game" of life. In the "game" of life, we are not only the spectators, but more importantly, we are the players and coaches as well. The fact is most of us live our lives just like The Glancer watches a football game—we get along by paying attention for a moment here or there, but we are usually "out of the room," thinking about other things. The goal of mindfulness training is to live more like The Watcher watches football. He observes closely each play of the game. The Watcher becomes so knowledgeable and familiar with the game of football simply because he is awake and attentive to what is happening in the game, play by play, as it takes place, game after game.

A football coach can understand what is happening in a football game, and make sound judgments and decisions in order to win that game, only to the extent that he is paying attention—that he is *awake and attentive* to what is actually happening, play by play, in the game. Imagine how absurd it would be if a coach spent the entire game, each week, *planning for next week's game!* Not only would he be ineffective in trying to win the *current* game, he would also be learning nothing that could be applied to winning *next week's* game—in other words, he would be absolutely worthless as a coach.

Well, the same principle applies to your life. *You can be effective—understand and affect what is happening in your life—only to the extent that you are awake and attentive to your present moment experience.* Being awake and attentive to the "game" of life—paying attention to your moment-to-moment experience—is essential to truly understand the "game", and thus be an effective "player/coach" in that "game."

VITAL SKILL

The Power of Mindfulness

The power of mindfulness, developed through the practice of bare attention, manifests itself in many ways. Following are five pertinent examples of how that power manifests to enhance personal effectiveness.

1. *Quieting the Mind:* When first beginning mindfulness practice, you will be deliberately observing, perhaps for the first time, the actual state of affairs in your mind. The level of "mental noise" that is encountered may be surprising.

> "Apart from the few main channels of his purposeful thoughts and activities, he will everywhere be faced with a tangled mass of perceptions, thoughts, feelings, casual bodily movements, etc., showing a disorderliness and confusion which he would certainly not tolerate, e.g., in his living room."
> (from Nyanaponika Thera, *The Power of Mindfulness*, p.7)

A mish-mash of random and disjointed thoughts, feelings, cravings, repulsions, emotions, longings, fantasies, daydreams, regrets, anxieties, and sense perceptions are there, all competing for your attention. Mental noise is like a veil, obscuring your ability to see the reality of the moment.

This chaotic condition is quieted and controlled by the practice of bare attention. The operative principle is the fact that your mind can have only one single object of attention at any given moment. If you sit quietly for a moment and observe what is going on in your mind, you will notice many different thoughts come and go. If you look carefully you will notice these thoughts occur one at a time, in succession, one after the other. Never do you have more than one thought in the same moment. In fact, if you deliberately *try* to attend to multiple thoughts in the same moment, you will find it to be impossible.

In practicing bare attention, your moment-to-moment experience becomes the object of attention, *displacing* the mental noise that is usually present. As mindfulness becomes stronger and more sustained, your moments become more and more consumed by present moment awareness, leaving less room for the mental noise to enter. When the mental noise does impose itself, as it tirelessly and tenaciously will, you direct your attention to *it*, recognizing and observing the noise itself as your present moment experience, and you begin to see it clearly for what it is—empty, boring, and valueless. Over time, with practice, the mental noise gradually weakens and fades, allowing you to be more present to what is actually going on in the moment.

Phil Jackson is a famous professional basketball player and coach, as well as a long-time practitioner and teacher of mindfulness. In his book, *Sacred Hoops*, he writes:

> "The more skilled I became at watching my thoughts in zazen [meditation] practice, the more focused I became as a player. I also developed an intimate knowledge of my mental processes on the basketball court.
>
> "My thoughts took many forms. There was pure self-interest… and selfless self-interest…. There was anger… and fear…. There was self-praise… and, more likely in my case, self-blame…. The litany was endless. However, the simple act of becoming mindful of the frenzied parade of thoughts, paradoxically, began to quiet my mind down."
>
> (from Phil Jackson, *Sacred Hoops*, p. 50)

2. *Labeling:* As you begin observing the contents of your mind, it will become apparent that you are, much of the time, being controlled by thought patterns—emotions, feelings, impulses—of which you are

entirely unaware, *but which often form the unexamined basis for choices, decisions and actions that directly affect your life.* Mindfulness has a penetrating quality that allows you to see this process more clearly.

For example, when you are fearful, for whatever reason, your normal reaction might be to flee from what is causing the fear, seek some form of external stimulation or distraction, or simply ignore the situation and try to suppress the fear. In these moments, it is fair to say that fear is in charge—it's as if you *are* fear, you are *being* fear, and fear is in control. Mindfulness helps you recognize what is going and regain control.

Mindfulness makes you aware of the presence of fear. You consciously recognize, "a fearful state of mind is present," or perhaps "fear-thoughts are present." The simple step of recognizing and *labeling* these thoughts as "fear-thoughts" has the almost magical effect of *disarming,* or *weakening* the fear that has hold of your mind. The grip of control that fear has over you is loosened. You have taken a "step back," *separating* yourself from the thoughts and feelings of fear.

With this "step back" you become more of an objective observer to what is going on. The experience is clearly recognized for what it is. You realize that you *are not* your fear—that the fear you are experiencing is based upon nothing more than a *thought.* A thought is just a thought—it has no basis in reality, it exists nowhere but in your mind, and it has no power or control in your life beyond what you give it.

When you recognize a fear-thought for what it is, just a *thought,* you are not so intimidated by it. The fear may not have vanished, but it has lost much of its power over you. You do not feel so compelled to be distracted away from it. You see that the fear is actually a *choice* that you have made, and that you are free to *re-choose.* Now you can face it directly, be with it, observe it, feel it, and learn something about its origin. With the penetrating quality of mindfulness, you see what beliefs or assumptions underlie and support the fear, and you can evaluate whether those beliefs and assumptions serve your best interest. Mindfulness converts a fearful episode into an opportunity for

VITAL SKILL

empowerment and insight. Whether it is fear, anger, lust, greed, self-doubt, confusion, hopelessness, or whatever, the principle remains the same. Mindfulness leads you toward empowerment and insight.

3. *Non-Judgement:* Mindfulness does not judge, and therefore it adds no stress or tension to your mental state. Mindfulness does not see things as good or bad, right or wrong, and is not concerned with taking corrective actions, changing things, or producing particular results. When you are free of judgement, you can accept each moment as it is, see all points of view, and all possibilities remain open to you.

4. *Conscious Pausing:* We have all had the experience of looking back at something we did or said, and thinking to ourselves: "What was I thinking when I said *that*?," or "Boy, was *that* dumb. I don't know what got into me." We impulsively speak or act without a thorough understanding of what is happening, how it relates to our desires and purpose, and before we know it, it is over and done. It is too late to reverse, and we have put ourselves in more of a mess than had we said or done nothing at all.

The practice of bare attention, by developing the capacity of conscious pausing, allows you to minimize or prevent these occasions where you act, react, speak, decide, choose, or conclude automatically and unconsciously.

> "In practicing bare attention, we *keep still* at the mental and spatial place of observation, amidst the loud demands of the inner and outer world. There is in it the strength of tranquility, the capacity of deferring action and applying the brake, of *stopping* rash interference, of suspending judgment while *pausing* for observation of facts and wise reflection on them. There is also a wholesome *slowing down* in the impetuosity of thought, speech and action."
> (Nyanaponika Thera, *The Power of Mindfulness*, p.25)

VITAL SKILL

Every action you perform is preceded by the *intention* to perform that action. As careful observation will verify, every action—from the most simple, seemingly automatic or reflexive action, like moving the hand to scratch an itch, to the most consequential actions you can think of—is preceded by the intention to perform that action. However most of the time this thought—i.e. *the intention*—goes entirely unnoticed, and before you know it the action has already taken place.

With mindfulness you gain the ability to be *conscious* in the moments preceding action, when your intentions are being formed. Thus you can *pause,* before acting, to examine your intentions and motivations, and the likely ramifications of what you intend. When you do act, you clearly comprehend what you are doing, and why, and you have a sense of the likely results. In this process you gain insight into what beliefs, habits, and assumptions are influencing your intentions, and thus your actions. The "force of habit" that controls so much of our normal, everyday interactions is brought more under control. Though this process may seem cumbersome, the reverse is actually true—with well-developed mindfulness it occurs effortlessly.

With the capacity of conscious pausing you will begin to appreciate, more and more, the wisdom of refraining from interference and involvement in every little thing going on around you. More frequently you will find yourself preferring, instead, to step back and let things play themselves out, somehow knowing this will ensure the best outcome for all involved. When you find, paradoxically, that you are often *more effective* when you seem to *do less*, I believe it signals that you are on the right track. From the Chinese book of wisdom, the *Tao Te Ching*:

> "Rushing into action, you fail.
> Trying to grasp things, you lose them.
> Forcing a project to completion,
> you ruin what was almost ripe.
> Therefore the Master takes action
> by letting things take their course.

He remains as calm
at the end as at the beginning...."
(from Stephen Mitchell, Tao Te Ching,
A New English Version, chapter 64)

5. *Directness of Vision:* With the practice of mindfulness you develop "directness of vision"—the ability to see things as they really are.

> "By directness of vision we understand a direct view of reality, without any coloring or distorting lenses, without the intrusion of emotional or habitual pre-judication and intellectual biases. It means coming face to face with the bare facts of actuality, seeing them as vivid and fresh as if they had occurred for the first time."
> (from Nyanaponika Thera, *The Power of Mindfulness*, p. 45)

To be truly effective you must see things, both within yourself, and out in the world, as they really are. Force of habit, beliefs, expectations, desires, past experience, a sense of urgency, fear, and mental confusion are some of the many factors that can prevent you, in the absence of mindfulness, from seeing clearly and directly what is before you in the present moment.

Factors That Impact Your Effectiveness

There are many factors that affect a person's ability to be effective in life. In this chapter I briefly discuss some that are particularly important, and how mindfulness affects these factors.

Beliefs

Your beliefs give rise to your view of the world. All of your perceptions, and how you feel and respond to all that you experience, are determined by your beliefs. Beliefs are omnipotent. They determine what you see as possible for yourself and what you feel you deserve and are capable of. Certain beliefs are not compatible with effectiveness, while other beliefs are critical for effectiveness. For example, if you believe you are not deserving or worthy of success and fulfillment, or that you are not good enough to succeed, or that it is somehow unfair or unjust for you to be successful, these are clearly beliefs that would limit your ability to produce the successful results you desire. On the other hand, it is obviously necessary for you to believe that you are capable and deserving of success, if you are to be successful.

No matter what skills, assets, or opportunities you may have access to, unconscious beliefs that lead to self-doubt, fear, anger, greed, refusal to accept responsibility, hopelessness, apathy, confusion, or other unhelpful mental states, will hinder your ability to be effective. Mindfulness of your beliefs enables you to see when your beliefs are a hindrance, identify those beliefs, and take corrective action if necessary.

It is through our interactions with the world, (i.e. our choices, decisions, perceptions, actions and reactions) that effectiveness is made real, and our beliefs are at the *core* of determining how we interact and engage with the world.

> "Parents, priests, teachers, corporate executives and politicians compete busily to teach us or sell us beliefs so that they can influence our feelings and behavior. They know, and we soon learn, that winning the games of power, both personal and political, depends on what we choose to believe. Nobel Prize winners, homemakers, army generals, secretaries, physicians, truck drivers, lawyers, masons, journalists, carpenters, advertising executives, have this in common: *they operate from their beliefs*. How they vote; what sort of army they support, if any; what purchases they make; where they live; whom they marry; what clothes they wear; *all flow from their beliefs*."
> (from *Happiness Is A Choice*, Barry Neil Kaufman, pp. 34-35)

One reason beliefs are so powerful is that they are always self-fulfilling, and therefore self-perpetuating. For example, suppose I have the belief that it is not possible for me to be successful (this is, in fact, a deeply held belief of my own that I have struggled with for many years). My actions, choices and decisions will be guided by this belief. I will behave in ways that reflect this belief, and I will strive, unconsciously, to create results that support, or fulfill this belief. These results, of course, serve to re-affirm, strengthen, and perpetuate the original belief.

I have found that when I have been headed toward a successful outcome, this belief has unconsciously motivated me to sabotage the potential success. In hindsight, I am aware of several instances where this has occurred over the years—where I have reached a point in some endeavor where success was imminent, only to suddenly lose interest, or become distracted by some other endeavor that was destined to lead nowhere. Mindfulness is the single element that has enabled me to realize what was going on, and to begin turning this limiting belief around. Fortunately, the self-fulfilling, self-perpetuating property of beliefs works equally well for positive, enabling beliefs as it does for limiting ones.

It is essential that we know our beliefs intimately, and see clearly how they act in our lives, if we are to realize true effectiveness. The problem is that in most cases our most fundamental beliefs—those that literally control our lives—are completely unconscious and unexamined. With practice, you will find one or two fundamental beliefs that are revealed over and over, in a wide range of different contexts. These are the basic core beliefs that dominate your life. These beliefs were formed in early childhood, and have rarely, if ever, been questioned. We unconsciously accept them as defining how the world works, even if they make absolutely no rational sense.

As you delve into this you may find that some of the things you believe about yourself, or about the world, are sabotaging your ability to be effective. You may even find that some of your most deeply held beliefs seem ridiculous when examined in the light of awareness. Identifying and getting to know these core beliefs, and witnessing how they control you, is extremely empowering.

Often there is a wide gap between what we consciously, or "intellectually" believe about ourselves and the world, and the deep-seated, unconscious core beliefs that actually guide our interactions. Mindfulness enables us to discover these unconscious core beliefs, making them conscious, so that we can examine them, understand them, and work to change them if we choose. The key is that mindfulness practice involves applying bare attention to our present moment thoughts, feelings, choices, decisions, and actions. In doing this we begin to see through to the beliefs and assumptions that *underlie* and *drive* those thoughts, feelings, choices, decisions and actions. With this awareness comes the opportunity to examine and evaluate our beliefs.

As we begin to see the beliefs that operate in our lives, it is helpful to be accepting of whatever beliefs we discover, even if we feel they are harmful or problematic for us in some way. We took them on in the first place because they served us at some point along the way;

but that was then, and this is now. If they are no longer beneficial to us, we can let them go or modify them. An attitude of acceptance allows us to keep unnecessary fear, anger, and frustration out of the picture, so that we can deal most effectively with any beliefs we wish to change or release.

Finally, we must realize that no beliefs are sacred, or universally true. There are no beliefs that should not be subject to questioning and examination. Simply put:

All beliefs are neutral—none are absolute.
We are free to choose beliefs that empower us, support us, and help us realize true effectiveness.

Fear

Fear deserves special mention because it is ubiquitous, and so potent in its ability to limit your effectiveness. Fear can work in a *million* different ways to prevent you from experiencing the fulfillment and success you seek.

Most of us, from the day we were born, have been immersed in fear. Fear permeates every aspect of our lives. Fear has countless clever disguises, and employs impeccable logic and reasoning to control our lives without our realizing it. The development of mindfulness is the only way we can begin to see clearly how fear operates in our lives.

Mindfulness helps you manage fear in two ways. First, with mindfulness, you are able to see fear in action, as it is acting. You begin to recognize fear behind its many costumes; e.g. "common sense," "good judgment," "wisdom," "caring and concern," and there are many more. You also begin to see how fear uses sound logic and reason to justify its agenda. While there are certainly times when fear is helpful for self-preservation, most often it is a crippling factor, limiting your view of life's possibilities and your ability to respond effectively to the challenges you face. True effectiveness requires mindfulness of fear acting in your life so that you can face it directly and move through it when appropriate.

Secondly, mindfulness is helpful because fear is only experienced in relation to thoughts about the future. It is your uncertainty about the future, and thoughts about all the bad, scary things that could happen in the future, that give rise to fear. As you develop mindfulness, and become more proficient at dwelling in the present moment, you find that fear does not exist when your awareness is anchored in the present moment. That is because there are no uncertainties in the present moment—everything is just as it is, and could not be any other way. Even if your present moment experience is difficult or undesirable, it is only when you *project* that experience into the future that you feel fear. Thinking about the future brings fear and anxiety, just as thinking about the past brings guilt and regret.

Unconscious beliefs and fear form the framework, or the boundaries, within which most of us live our lives. Mindfulness allows us to live, instead, according to our heart's desires and life purpose.

Worry

One thing you end up with when beliefs combine with fear is *worry*. I believe it was Mark Twain who once said: "I've dealt with a lot of hardship in my life, most of which never happened." It is fair to say that many of us are addicted to worry:

—We feel we have problems, and believe that worrying about those problems will help us find solutions.

—We are concerned about the future, and worrying may give us the illusion of a sense of control over what will happen in the future.

—We believe we are inadequate, not good enough, and that we can somehow make up for that by worrying.

—There are a lot of things we believe we *should* do, are *supposed* to do, or *must do to be safe*—but that we do not particularly *want*

to do. Worrying may be the only way we can motivate ourselves to do these things.
—Fear tells us the world is not safe, and that if we do not remain vigilant, by worrying, we will leave ourselves vulnerable, or our lives will fall apart—as though our worrying will protect us from bad things happening.

Once you buy into worrying, there is no end to the things you can worry about—there are problems to solve, answers to figure out, plans to make, past mistakes to regret and feel guilty about, goals to achieve, future challenges to prepare for, deadlines to meet, endless uncertainties to feel anxious about, and so on.

Mindfulness would have you loosen your grip on worry, and direct your attention to what is happening in the present moment. However, if you are addicted to worry, this can be very difficult. Usually, whatever it is you are worrying about seems more relevant, or more urgent, than what is actually happening in the present moment. Fear won't allow you to "trust" the present moment. Fear makes it seem that if you let go of worry, and direct your attention to what is here before you, you would be irresponsible, or neglectful of something more important, and would therefore be putting yourself at risk. But in truth there is nothing more relevant, urgent, important, or more *trustworthy*, than the present moment experience.

That is not to say that there is never cause to be concerned about situations, problems, or events that are not related to what is happening right in front of you, in the present moment. But what is important, when worry has a hold of your mind, is that you consciously recognize that *worry itself is your present moment experience*, and that whatever you are worrying about is being viewed from a frame of reference defined by unconscious beliefs and fear.

With mindfulness you can step back, separate yourself from the worry, and ground yourself in the here and now. You see how your beliefs and fears are contributing to worry. You recognize that worry has a certain bodily sensation associated with it—the same bodily sensation that fear brings because worry *is* fear. (This sensation is an effective indicator to alert you when fear is acting.) You also see the fact that your worrying is not having any positive impact on whatever it is you are worrying about. Efforts to control life, by worrying, are completely ineffective. With the development of mindfulness, you can reduce the role of worry in your life.

Stress

Stress is a universal factor that can dramatically affect your ability to be effective in life. Mindfulness lies at the very heart of effectively dealing with stress.

Stress is a vast and complex subject which, at the risk of over-simplifying, we will discuss briefly. We can view stress in the way first proposed by Dr. Hans Selye in the 1950's. Dr. Selye defined *stress* as *the total, non-specific response, or reaction (including both mind and/or body) of an organism to any pressure or demand.* (Jon Kabat-Zin, *Full Catastrophe Living*) Selye also coined the term *stressor*, to refer to *any stimulus—event, condition, circumstance—that produces a stress response or reaction in the individual. A* stressor can originate from an *internal* or an *external* stimulus. Examples of internal stressors are illness, disease, as well as fear and limiting or negative beliefs. Common external stressors might be job pressures, financial pressures, physical environment (extreme temperatures), physical injury or pain, and there are countless more.

Stressors are present over the entire range of severity—from lethal forces like highly toxic substances or destructive physical impact, to largely benign forces that may go unnoticed by most of us, like gravity, noise, or light, and everything in between. It is the vast array of stressors in the middle range that we address in this discussion. These are the stressors that are faced by all of us on a daily basis, and though not immediately harmful, if not dealt with effectively, they can be devastating over the course of a lifetime.

Another useful way that stress is commonly defined is as *a particular relationship between the person and the environment that is appraised by the person as taxing, or exceeding his or her resources, and endangering his or her well-being.* This definition drives home the important fact that, while stress is a universal condition, every individual experiences it in their *own individual* way. Put another way, events, conditions, or circumstances that are very stressful to *me* may not be the least bit stressful to *you*, and vice-versa. While there are certainly some stressors that would produce stress in almost anyone, there is no definitive universal listing of what causes stress and what does not. A person's *perception* and *appraisal* of what is happening is the key to determining his or her reaction or response, and therefore the amount of stress experienced.

Jon Kabat-Zinn, Ph.D, is the founder of The Mindfulness Based Stress Reduction Center at the University of Massachusetts Medical Center, and author of the authoritative book on treating stress with mindfulness practice, *Full Catastrophe Living*. In his book, he makes the critical distinction between *reacting* vs. *responding* to events, conditions, and circumstances in life (potential stressors), and the corresponding effects in the formation of stress. It is in this distinction that the fundamental importance of mindfulness, moment-to-moment awareness, in effectively dealing with stress becomes evident.

"Reacting" to Stressors

Dr. Kabat-Zinn uses the term *stress reactivity* to describe the pattern of *unconscious, automatic* reaction to stressors. This is the pattern in which we find ourselves when we suddenly recognize we are experiencing excessive or debilitating levels of stress in our lives. The key words here are *unconscious* and *automatic*—this pattern is created and perpetuated by a lack of mindfulness. In this pattern, we are not consciously *aware* that the stressors are present, nor are we conscious of our *perception* and *appraisal* of the stressors. It is our resulting *unconscious, automatic* reactions to those stressors that determine the level of stress we experience. This is a cyclic pattern that insidiously feeds on itself—fulfilling and perpetuating itself without our awareness. Dr. Kabat-Zinn writes:

> "Automatic reactions, triggered out of unawareness, usually compound and exacerbate stress, making what might have remained basically simple problems into worse ones. They prevent us from seeing clearly, from solving problems creatively, from expressing our emotions effectively when we need to communicate with other people, and ultimately they prevent us from attaining peace of mind. Instead, each time we react, we stress our intrinsic balance even more. A lifetime of unconscious reactivity is likely to increase our risk of eventual breakdown and illness significantly."
>
> (from Jon Kabat-Zinn, *Full Catastrophe Living*, p. 248)

When stressors are encountered, stress reactivity is generally characterized by some sort of *alarm reaction*, a common example being the *fight-or-flight reaction*. An *alarm reaction*, in whatever form, can range from very mild to very severe. It typically involves psychological and physiological *hyper-arousal*, resulting in some mix of strong emotions, excessive muscle tension, and a whole string of nervous-system responses that can dramatically affect your physical and mental state. If left unchecked over time, stress reactivity can lead to *disregulation* (e.g. high blood pressure, sleep disorders, chronic headaches, back pain, anxiety), *maladaptive coping* (e.g. self-destructive behaviors, overworking, hyperactivity, overeating, denial), *substance dependency* (e.g. drugs, alcohol, tobacco, caffeine, food), and ultimately *breakdown* (e.g. physical/psychological exhaustion, depression, heart attack, cancer).

"Responding" to Stressors

The key to dealing effectively with stress lies in consciously *responding* to stressors, rather than unconsciously and automatically *reacting* to stressors. Dr. Kabat-Zinn writes:

> "And so we come back to the key importance of mindfulness. The very first and most important step in breaking free from a lifetime of stress reactivity is to be mindful of what is actually

happening while it is happening." (from Jon Kabat-Zinn, *Full Catastrophe Living*, p. 264)

Mindfulness allows us to employ the elements of *choice* and *control*, starting at the moment stressors are encountered. Mindfulness makes us aware of the stressors in the moment, as they are acting. We see our automatic stress reactivity kicking in, but in that moment we can assess what is going on, and there is the opportunity to choose differently—to *not* allow our automatic reactions to take over. We are mindful of our thoughts, feelings, external threats, and of our perception and appraisal of those threats. We can see how our own fear and beliefs are influencing the automatic reaction that we see taking place. If we are agitated, we can consciously relax and calm ourselves. Mindfulness allows us to see clearly the full context of our situation, and to be aware of our overriding intentions, goals, desires, and any other relevant factors in the moment.

Being mindful does not mean you will respond in some specific way every time you face stressors, but rather, it increases the likelihood that you will respond most *appropriately* for the particular situation.

"When you are grounded in calmness and moment-to-moment awareness, you are more likely to be creative and to see new options, new solutions to problems. You are more likely to be aware of your emotions and less likely to be carried away by them. It will be easier for you to maintain your balance and sense of perspective in trying circumstances."
(from Jon Kabat-Zinn, *Full Catastrophe Living*, p. 269)

Acceptance

An important aspect of mindfulness is open acceptance of the present moment reality. We have already discussed how expectations, conditions and judgements can make it difficult to accept the present moment as it is. In addition, true acceptance requires letting go of three things:

<u>Blame</u>: We must let go of the need to blame others when things are not as we would like. Blame is never beneficial. It prevents us from taking responsibility for our situation, and from facing the issues that must be addressed to bring about positive change.
<u>Playing the victim</u>: We must let go of the need to play the victim. Playing the role of the victim is similar to blaming—it is refusing to take responsibility for what is happening in our lives, and preventing ourselves from facing the issues in our lives that need to be addressed.
<u>Comparing</u>: We must break the habit of comparing ourselves to others in order to judge how we are doing. If we compare to someone who has less than we have, it feels good. If we compare to someone who has more than we have, it feels lousy. But in no case is comparison ever beneficial. We must accept ourselves right where we are in the present moment.

Many of us fear that if we openly accept present moment conditions that we don't like, we will have no motivation to change things in the future—as though dissatisfaction, discontentment, and worry are necessary motivators for us to work to make our lives better. In fact the opposite is true.

> "Some people worry that happiness [i.e. people happily accepting their present moment circumstances, abandoning dissatisfaction, discontentment and worry] and lethargy go hand in hand, as if happy people would be without motivation to initiate or participate in human endeavors. Since the cup of happiness would be filled, they reason, we would have no motivation to do anything further. Not so! Instead of using anger, fear, discomfort or jealousy as fuel for action, we would energize ourselves with peace, ease, comfort and excitement, and have more reason than ever before to involve ourselves in the pursuits we choose. The

happy skier glides more easily down the slope than her fearful counterpart. The happy musician delights enthusiastically in the music he plays, while the tense artist short-circuits his efforts by fatigue or distress. The happy teacher enjoys passionately the curiosity, the struggles and the victories of her students while her judgmental colleague burns out on her own impatience and annoyance in the classroom. Happy people do not stop moving or participating. On the contrary, their happiness increases their mobility and effectiveness. Instead of fighting fears and running from pain, they see more clearly their wants and move with ease toward them."

(from Barry Neil Kaufman, *Happiness is a Choice*, p. 67)

Awareness of our heart's desires and life purpose is the best motivator that we have for working toward positive change. Dissatisfaction, discontentment and worry are distractions from the present moment experience. With acceptance of the present moment, we are free to address the present moment situation, to see clearly our heart's desire and life purpose, and to act most appropriately to realize our goals.

Consequences

Nothing ever actually *happens* in a past moment. Things *did happen* in past moments, but at the moment they happened, it was the *present* moment. We do not have the ability to reach back and change past moments. Once a moment has happened, it is gone; we have no power or control over that moment. Likewise with future moments, things *will happen* in future moments, but it will be the *present* moment when they happen. We really don't know what will happen in future moments, nor do we have the ability to control or manipulate what will happen in future moments.

We can recall or think about past moments, but we can't touch them, change them, or re-live them. We can anticipate or think about

VITAL SKILL

future moments, but we can't touch them, control them, or dictate just what will happen when they arrive. Indeed we could say that past and future moments don't actually exist except in our minds, but we do have a connection to them. We are connected to both past and future moments, in the present moment, through *consequences*.

In the present moment we are unavoidably faced with the consequences of our past actions, choices and decisions. And consequences of the actions, choices and decisions of the present moment will unavoidably be with us in the future. The important point is that all consequences result from actions, choices and decisions made in the *present moment*. Consequences from unwise actions can be long lasting and have a direct impact on our lives. If our present moments are lived without attention and awareness, the consequences we will face in the future are entirely out of our control.

For many of us, our present "life situation" is almost entirely shaped by the *consequences* of past moments lived without awareness. With mindfulness, we have more control over our present moment interactions, and thus the consequences that result.

VITAL SKILL

The Mindfulness Faculties of Effectiveness

We have defined mindfulness and effectiveness, and have talked about how they are connected through The First Law of Effectiveness. We have talked about the present moment orientation, the essence of mindfulness (bare attention), the power of mindfulness, and the effects of mindfulness on various effectiveness factors. While the actual practice of mindfulness is ultimately very simple, resting on the simple practice of bare attention, it is clear that the effects and benefits of the practice are numerous and far-reaching.

We can view the practice of mindfulness as a form of mental training. In order to perform at peak levels, an athlete must train his/her body—developing strong, flexible muscles and bones, and honing specific skills and reflexes. Similarly, true effectiveness in life requires that we train our minds. Over thousands of years, the practice of mindfulness has proven an extremely powerful method of training the mind. The effects and benefits of mindfulness practice, as related to personal effectiveness, can be summed up by introducing what I call the Mindfulness Faculties of Effectiveness, *Clear Perception*, *Clear Recollection*, and *Presence of Mind*. These faculties arise through mindfulness practice, and together form the *foundation* of true effectiveness:

1. *Clear Perception* is the ability to clearly perceive the true nature of what is going on both outside and inside ourselves, and how they are related, in the present moment. It means seeing through the surface appearance of external situations and events, and grasping the essential truth of what is happening in the moment, without interference from desires or expectations. It provides insight as to why things are happening as they are, and how they are related to

VITAL SKILL

other events and situations. Clear Perception keeps us from being swept away by our feelings, emotions, thoughts, and desires. It allows us to see them for what they are, and gives us the ability to recognize the forces that underlie and drive them— e.g. beliefs, love, fear. Clear Perception, through present moment awareness of our feelings, emotions, thoughts, and desires, is the key to clearly perceiving our true heart's desires and life purpose, thus making *true* effectiveness possible.

2. *Clear Recollection* is the clear, present moment awareness of your heart's desires and life purpose. It is the faculty that enables you to keep your eye on the *big picture*. Clear Recollection enables you to view your thoughts, feelings, actions, choices and decisions; your goals, aspirations, intentions, and efforts; and the external events and situations of the present moment—all seen via Clear Perception—as they relate to your heart's desires and life purpose. Clear Recollection also makes relevant knowledge and understanding available for use in the present moment.

> "Mindfulness helps us keep our personal purpose in front of us. Mindfulness makes it possible to see the goals that are implied by our personal purpose. Mindfulness keeps us informed of the necessity and the results of persistence, of facing the facts [of our present moment situation, and] of minimizing our risks [i.e. proceeding with attention]."
>
> (from Claude Whitmyer, *Mindfulness and Meaningful Work*, p. 257)

3. *Presence of Mind* means you are *right here, right now*, with your attention, awareness, and consciousness in the present moment, where effectiveness, and life itself, takes place. It enables you to utilize clear perception and clear recollection to take the appropriate actions, choices, and decisions (interactions with the world) in the moment. Presence of Mind allows you to make wise use of your creativity, intuition, impulses, insight, and inspirations—these

VITAL SKILL

are powerful allies, available only through present moment awareness, which can help you find the ideas, answers, and solutions you need. It enables you to recognize and seize opportunities and open doors as they present themselves. Presence of mind is the faculty that is needed for you to do what must be done, in the moment, to move yourself in the direction of fulfillment and success.

No matter what area of life or specific endeavor, these three mindfulness faculties are the keys to true personal effectiveness. You need to see the essence of what is happening both inside and outside, in the moment. You must be cognizant of your heart's desires and life purpose, and have ready access to relevant knowledge and understanding in the moment. And you must be present to the situations of your life, to be able to take appropriate action and make wise choices and decisions, in the moment. (Fig. 10)

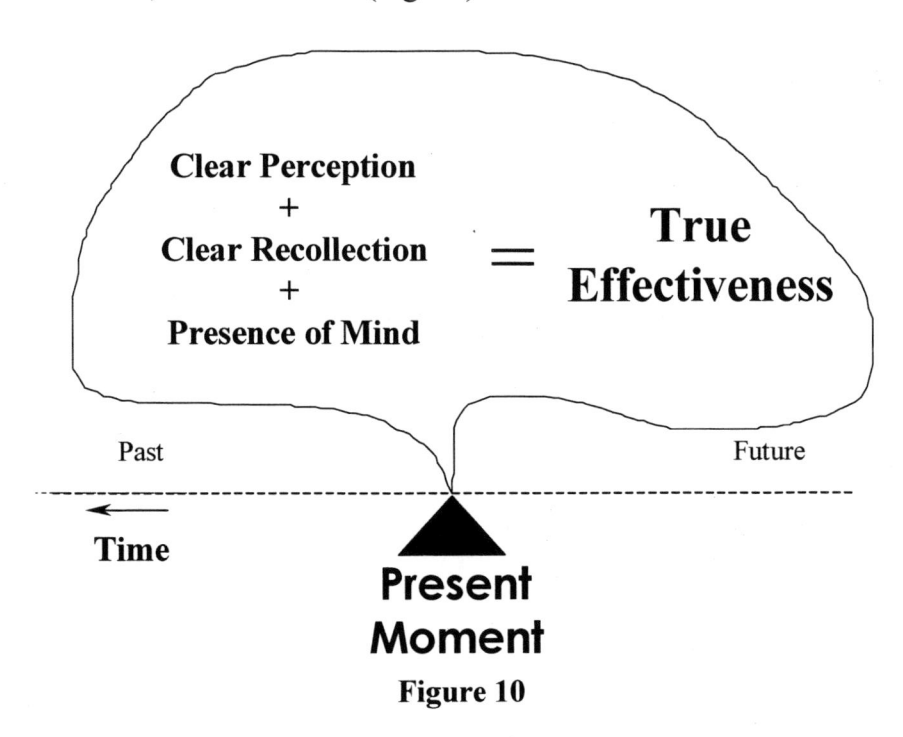

Clear Perception + Clear Recollection + Presence of Mind = True Effectiveness

Past ← Time → Future

Present Moment

Figure 10

The Coach

Phil Jackson was head coach of the Chicago Bulls basketball team during the 1990's, when they won six NBA championships. In his book, *Sacred Hoops*, Jackson reveals himself to be a long-time, devoted practitioner and teacher of mindfulness. The practice of mindfulness lies at the very heart of his approach to life, as well as his approach to coaching basketball. He writes:

> "Basketball is a complex dance that requires shifting from one objective to another at lightning speed. To excel, you need to act with a clear mind and be totally focused on what everyone on the floor is doing.... What you really need to do is become more acutely aware of what's happening right now, this very moment.... The point is to perform every activity, from playing basketball to taking out the garbage, with precise attention, moment to moment."
>
> (from Phil Jackson, *Sacred Hoops*, pp. 115-116)

Coach Jackson sees mindfulness as the key not only to getting the highest level of individual performance from his players, but also, and more importantly, the key to enabling them to play as a unified team, with the unified goal of playing with integrity and compassion, and winning. Let's apply the Mindfulness Faculties of Effectiveness—Clear Perception, Clear Recollection, and Presence of Mind—to see how they might help produce the results he sought to achieve:

<u>Clear perception:</u> It is essential for the players to see clearly what is going on in the present moment, during the game. They must know what's happening on the floor, where each player is, how much time is left. They must recognize when their own thoughts, feelings, choices, decisions, and actions may be in conflict, or an impediment to the team goal of winning the game. They must also see clearly what their opponents are up to—e.g. what tactics they are using to win the game.

VITAL SKILL

As an example, one of Jackson's challenges during his championship years coaching the Bulls was dealing with teams that used excessive violence as a tactic for winning:

> "It was no coincidence that the players had a hard time staying focused against [the] Detroit [Pistons]. The Piston's primary objective was to throw us off our game by raising the level of violence on the floor. They pounded away at the players ruthlessly, pushing, shoving, sometimes even head-butting, to provoke them into retaliating. As soon as that happened [i.e. retaliation], the battle was over."
>
> (from Phil Jackson, *Sacred Hoops,* p. 132)

Jackson's goal was to teach his players to respond to this treatment not out of anger or hatred toward the opponent, but rather out of a sense of respect and compassion for the contest, and for the opponent as well. Clear perception enabled his players to perceive this rough treatment accurately—not as a personal challenge or attack, as it would appear on the surface, but rather, as a desperate tactic employed by an intensely competitive opponent, to try to win the game. This awareness, in the midst of the "battle," increased their ability to tolerate the rough play while staying focused on their unified goal—playing their best team-basketball, and *winning*—rather than responding out of anger and trying to get even.

<u>Clear Recollection:</u> To be successful on Jackson's team, the players needed to be cognizant, in the present moment, of *why* they were there—of what was their goal, purpose, or reason for being a member of that team. They also had to be aware, in the moment, of their particular role in reaching that goal within the confines of the overall team strategy. In this particular case the overriding goal, or purpose for each player was to be a pure team player—to put their individual needs and desires second to those of the team. The unique offensive strategy Jackson was implementing required a total commitment from each

player to the team goal of winning games by playing superior basketball, *as a team*. He writes:

> "This is the struggle every leader faces: how to get members of the team who are driven by the quest for individual glory to give themselves over wholeheartedly to the group effort. In other words, how to teach them selflessness.
>
> "In basketball, this is an especially tricky problem. Today's NBA players have a dazzling array of individual moves, most of which they've learned from coaches who encourage one-on-one play. In an effort to become "stars," young players will do almost anything to draw attention to themselves, to say 'This is me' with the ball, rather than share the limelight with others. The skewed reward system in the NBA only makes matters worse.... As a result, few players come to the NBA dreaming of becoming good team players."
>
> (from Phil Jackson, *Sacred Hoops*, pp. 89-90)

Ultimately mindfulness—clear recollection—was the key that enabled the players to effectively and consistently, game after game, execute this unique strategy. Jackson credits this strategy in large part for the team's tremendous success.

<u>Presence of Mind:</u> Presence of mind is the ability to integrate clear perception and clear recollection, in the present moment, to produce right, appropriate present moment action. This is a spontaneous, present moment phenomenon that does not involve thinking. Jackson experienced the value of presence of mind in his days as a player:

> "The key [for the basketball player] is seeing and doing. If you're focusing on anything other that reading the court and doing what needs to be done, the moment will pass you by.

VITAL SKILL

"Sitting zazen [seated mindfulness practice], I learned to *trust the moment*—to immerse myself in action as mindfully as possible, so that I could react spontaneously to whatever was taking place. When I played without 'putting a head on top of a head,' as one Zen teacher puts it, I found that my true nature as an athlete emerged."

(from Phil Jackson, *Sacred Hoops*, pp. 50-51)

For the basketball player, in the midst of a game, presence of mind means doing the right thing—move, pass, shoot—at the right time. As for the rest of us, in the midst of the various situations and challenges we face in everyday life, presence of mind is the key for us as well, to doing the right thing at the right time.

VITAL SKILL

Part II

VITAL SKILL

Part I focused mainly on what mindfulness is, how it is related to effectiveness, and why it is so important to each one of us. This is all very important because it forms the basis for conviction and commitment, the first two requirements for developing any skill. In Part II we focus on the third requirement, practice.

I use the analogy of writing a book about playing piano. If I wrote a good book about playing the piano, and you read it, you might get a sense of what it is like to be a good piano player. You would begin to understand the joy, excitement, and fulfillment of being able to sit down at the piano and play a piece of beautiful music with your own two hands. By the time you finished the book, if I had done a good job, you might feel a great desire to learn to play piano—you might even feel that learning to play piano was the most valuable thing you could do for yourself. But after finishing the book, no matter how you felt about playing piano, you would be no closer to being able to actually *play* the piano than you were before reading the book. You may have arrived at conviction and commitment to the idea of learning to play, but the key component of practice (not to mention some instruction) would be essential if you wanted to actually play the piano.

The Practice of Mindfulness

Practice is the only way to develop mindfulness. Mindfulness practice is not a quick fix for anything, but it is the necessary starting point for creating true personal effectiveness. It is not a "learning" process as much as it is an "awakening" and "un-learning" process. It facilitates the recognition of a lifetime of conditioning that constantly operates outside our awareness. Mindfulness takes time and effort to develop, and its value can be realized only through one's own practice and experience. Before getting into the exercises themselves, I will touch on some basic ideas that underlie mindfulness practice.

Objects of Mindfulness

To practice bare attention, we first must know what we are going to pay attention *to*. Even when there is not a lot going on around us, there is an awful lot we can observe within. To categorize the various aspects of the present moment experience that can be observed, Buddhist doctrine outlines *The Four Objects of Mindfulness* as follows (very briefly):

1. Mindfulness of the Body: This is mindfulness of what is happening specifically with our body in the moment. Some examples are mindfulness of breath, posture, body position, parts of the body, and bodily movement or action.

2. Mindfulness of Feelings: This is mindfulness of what we are feeling, feelings of both physical (as conveyed by the five physical senses) and mental origin (conveyed by the sixth sense, mind), in the moment. The main focus here is the experiencing of the feeling, its recognition as "pleasant," "unpleasant," or "neutral," and as being based either in the body or the mind.

3. Mindfulness of Mental State: This is mindfulness of our state of mind, which describes the general "color," "tone," or underlying quality of our thoughts and feelings, in the moment. Some examples of mental states are anger, lust, greed, jubilation, satisfaction, fear, self-confidence, stress, calmness, and confusion. We consciously recognize our mental state, realizing it does not define *who we are*—it is not *me*, *I*, or *self*—it is just the state of our consciousness in the moment.

4. Mindfulness of Mental Contents: This is mindfulness of specific mental states or objects of attention, with cognizance of how they are identified and categorized in Buddhist philosophy.

Levels of Awareness

Mindfulness combines awareness of the present moment experience at two levels—the level of *experience* and the level of *cognition*:

1. <u>Awareness at the Level of Experience</u>: At the level of experience we directly and fully *experience* what is happening in the moment. Our attention is focused on the experience itself—i.e. the *feelings* associated with the experience, both physical and mental—without the intrusion of ideas and concepts *about* the experience. Example: When you are sitting, you focus attention on the sensations and feelings, both prominent and subtle, associated with sitting; e.g. feelings of touch or pressure of your body against the chair. When you are walking, you focus attention on the sensations and feelings associated with walking; e.g. pressure of the feet against the ground, or movement of the legs with each step. When you are aware of a fearful state of mind, you focus attention on the sensations and feelings that accompany the mental state of fear; e.g. that hollow, empty, "pit-like" feeling in the stomach, excessive muscle tension in the neck and shoulders, or perhaps racing thoughts and a sense of panic.

2. <u>Awareness at the Level of Cognition</u>: At the level of cognition, we "*step back*" from experiencing, and become *cognizant* of—i.e. we consciously *recognize*—what is happening in the moment. The idea is to clearly recognize and comprehend what the present moment experience is—what we are doing, why we are doing it, and what is *actually happening*, inside and outside of ourselves, here and now. This is generally practiced by consciously *identifying and labeling* the experience, or object of attention of the moment. Example: When you are sitting, you consciously recognize: "sitting." When you are walking, you consciously recognize: "walking." Or if you are walking to the store, you consciously recognize: "walking to the store." When you feel tired, you consciously recognize: "feeling tired." When you

are angry, you consciously recognize: "anger is present," or "feeling angry," and so on.

As an example, consider the activity of driving a car. While driving a car, awareness at the level of experience would mean that you *experience* what is happening in the present moment as you are driving; you hear the road noise, you *smell* the car exhaust, you *feel* the air temperature, the wind swirling around (if the window is open), the car seat against your body, your posture, and the subtle movements of your hands and feet as you drive. Along with that, at the level of cognition, you are *cognizant* of the fact that you are driving your car ("driving my car"), of where you are ("on I-95 North"), where you are *going*, and why ("headed to the office for a meeting"), whether you are cold or hot ("feeling hot"), your feeling ("nervous about the upcoming meeting"), the weather and road conditions ("it's raining, roads are slippery"), and so on.

The mindfulness exercises we practice develop the ability to directly *experience* our present moment experience, and remain *cognizant* of what that experience is—what is happening, what we are doing, what we are feeling. This is one of the unique and powerful aspects of mindfulness training. The result for the practitioner is an increased sense of wakefulness, clarity, calm and stability—these qualities are maximized through the practice of mindfulness.

Approach to Practice

The general approach to practice has two aspects, which I call "dedicated practice" and "on-going practice." These two aspects are equally important and compliment each other quite well. Both must be developed to create a strong daily practice.

Dedicated Practice: In dedicated practice we set aside some time each day, when the demands from the world are minimal, and devote this time to the practice of bare attention. This is where we develop

VITAL SKILL

our power of concentration—the ability to apply bare attention on a sustained, moment-to-moment basis. Ideal times of the day for dedicated practice are mornings and evenings. The main challenge of dedicated practice is *making time* each day to do it.

On-Going Practice: In on-going practice, throughout the day we apply bare attention to our activities, thoughts, feelings, etc., wherever and whenever possible. This is where we practice mindfulness within the context of the situations, events, and challenges of our everyday life. The main challenge of on-going practice is *remembering* to do it each day.

VITAL SKILL

Practice Exercises

Below, I present a set of basic exercises that can be adapted and used by anyone for the purpose of developing mindfulness. Do not get bogged down when reading through these exercises—there is no need to memorize them. There are countless ways that mindfulness can be practiced, and many of the exercises presented here will not work for everyone. What follows are practice ideas that have worked well for me. Later in the book we discuss how to make use of these exercises to develop a daily practice.

Conscious Breathing

Your biggest ally in the practice of mindfulness is your breath. The breath serves as both an *anchor*, to keep you in the present moment, and a *tether* that you can grab on to, to pull yourself *back* to the present moment when your mind has wandered off. Your breath is always with you, and is an ever-present link to the present moment reality. When you are mindful of your breathing, you are connected to the present moment, where life is taking place. Awareness of the breath also connects you to the miraculous life force that ensures that your breathing, heartbeat, and other life supporting functions continue, keeping you alive, without any conscious effort or concern on your part. I recommend that you forge a new, intimate relationship with your breath, and make it the foundation of your mindfulness practice.

Dedicated Practice Exercises Using the Breath

Breathing is an on-going, endless process that is a perfect object of observation for practicing bare attention. Presented here are five basic meditation exercises for daily, dedicated mindfulness practice, which focus on awareness of the breath. These exercises can be performed in a seated or lying position (a seated position is preferred since it leaves one less vulnerable to sleepiness). Sitting cross-legged on the floor, with a small cushion under the buttocks, or sitting on a comfortable chair, with feet on the floor is fine. The important thing is to sit upright, with back and neck "straight" (imagine the crown of your head is being gently pulled upward), hands resting on thighs, and with eyes closed or gazing gently downward at about 45 degrees. Breathe through the nose, making no effort to control or modify the breath. In these exercises we do not practice any special kind of *breathing*, we simply practice *observing* our normal breathing. To start out, I suggest practicing for 5-10 minutes at a time, twice daily. The best times are morning and evening, though anytime is fine. Gradually increase the practice periods to 30 minutes or more.

1. <u>Counting the Breath</u>: This exercise is performed seated, breathing normally, with no effort to control or modify the breath. The object is to count successive breaths, from "one—ten." When "ten" is reached, start again at "one." Repeat this cycle for the duration of the practice period. This is an excellent beginning exercise for developing your power of concentration. Practice as follows:
- When breathing in, consciously count, "one, one, one…"
- When breathing out, consciously count, "one, one, one…"
- When breathing in, consciously count, "two, two, two…"
- When breathing out, consciously count, "two, two, two…"
- When breathing in, consciously count, "three, three, three…"
- When breathing out, consciously count, "three, three, three…"
 … and so on, until "ten" is reached.
Repeat for the duration of the practice period.

If the count is lost, or breaths skipped along the way, do not try to pick up where you left off, but rather start over again at "one," consciously recognizing, "starting over."

2. <u>Following the Breath:</u> Again, this exercise is performed seated, breathing normally, with no effort to control or modify the breath. The object here is to consciously *follow*—i.e. maintain moment-to-moment awareness of—the "in-breath" and "out-breath." Practice as follows:
- When breathing in, consciously recognize, "breathing in, breathing in…"
- When breathing out, consciously recognize, "breathing out, breathing out…"
- Repeat for the duration of the practice period.

3. Exercise #2 can be enhanced by consciously recognizing the "top" and "bottom" of each breath. The "top" of the breath is the transition point at which the in-breath ends, and the out-breath begins. The "bottom" of the breath is the transition point at which the out-breath ends, and the in-breath begins. At "top" and "bottom" there is a moment where there is no in-breath or out-breath; that is the point recognized as the transition point. Practice as follows:
- When breathing in, consciously recognize, "breathing in, breathing in…"
- At the top of the breath, consciously recognize, "top"
- When breathing out, consciously recognize, "breathing out, breathing out…"
- At the bottom of the breath, consciously recognize, "bottom"
- Repeat for the duration of the practice period.

4. <u>Experiencing the breath:</u> Exercises #1–#3 operate primarily at the level of *cognition*. These exercises can be modified to shift awareness to the *experience* level. Here, the object of attention is the rising and falling of the abdomen, which occurs with normal breathing. To practice this exercise, focus attention on the feelings and sensations associated with the rising and falling of the abdomen as breathing takes

place. You might focus on the feeling of movement of the abdomen against your clothes, or perhaps the feeling of expansion and contraction of the abdomen from within. If it is difficult to sense this at first, place your hand gently on the abdomen to focus your awareness to that area. Practice one breath at a time, the goal being to stay focused on the abdomen, moment-to-moment, for the entire breath (i.e. the full in-out cycle). Keep your attention focused on experiencing the movement of the abdomen continuously, breath after breath, for the duration of the practice period.

5. While practicing these exercises you may notice an array of visual images passing through your mind. The visualizing faculty of your mind can be a major source of distraction, attracting your attention and pulling you into endless daydreams and fantasies. The best way to deal with this is to deliberately *engage* your visualizing faculty as part of the practice exercise. Exercise #4 can be modified to accomplish this. Here again, the object of attention is the rising and falling of the abdomen. This time, in addition to being aware of the feelings and sensations, as in exercise #4, you also *visualize* the rising and falling of the abdomen, as you breathe. With the in-breath, visualize the abdomen rising, and with the out-breath, visualize the abdomen falling. Exactly what the image is that you "see" is not important. You will find that the image in your "mind's eye" follows your awareness of the feelings and sensations of breathing. Simply establish the intention to visualize the rising and falling of the abdomen, focus your attention on the abdomen, and observe whatever image the mind presents as you breathe.

A Few Pointers

All of these exercises are very simple, but not necessarily easy, especially in the beginning. Following are some pointers, which apply to the dedicated, seated practice techniques of exercises #1–#5 above, that may help you deal with common obstacles.

Shortness of Breath

In the above exercises, breathe just as you would in a very relaxed state. If you experience a feeling of shortness of breath in exercises #1–#5, try breathing in deeply, then breathing out completely, constricting the abdomen to expel as much air as possible. Repeat this a few times as follows:

- When breathing in deeply, consciously recognize, "breathing in deeply"
- When breathing out completely, consciously recognize, "breathing out completely"
- Repeat a few times and resume the exercise being practiced.

Also, focus your attention on your abdomen. In normal, unrestricted breathing, most of the in-out movement should be in the abdomen rather than the chest, as if the air travels down *through* the chest, into the abdomen. It is common to hold tension in the abdomen, which restricts natural, easy, deep breathing. Are you holding tension in the abdominal area? For example, you may find that you unconsciously "hold in" your abdomen, as if trying to appear to have a "flat belly"—this makes comfortable breathing impossible. To breathe well you must release your abdomen completely. This may feel odd, or even uneasy at first because you are so used to holding tension there, but it is essential. You will probably find that the tension returns immediately when your attention is diverted—but stay with it.

You could even make an entire practice of simply monitoring and releasing tension in the abdomen as you breathe. Think of it as "softening" the abdomen to allow the breathing to take place there. Before long releasing this tension will feel very natural and will produce a feeling of calm and well-being. Practice as follows:

- If you are holding tension, consciously recognize, "holding tension"
- As you release the tension, consciously recognize, "releasing tension"
- Resume the exercise being practiced.

Distraction

Do not be discouraged or frustrated when distracted during practice. Distraction is a normal and natural part of mindfulness practice. Distraction, in the form of sleepiness, daydreaming, fantasizing, worrying, physical discomfort, thinking about... whatever, goes with the territory. Remember that most of us have spent the majority of our lives distracted from the present moment. It's not an easy habit to break.

When distraction occurs, the trick is first to *awaken* from the distraction, recognize it, acknowledge it, and then gently but firmly return to the exercise being practiced. Resist the urge to participate or get wrapped up in the distraction. Do not judge the distraction, and do not judge yourself for being distracted.

It is through the process of repeatedly awakening from distractions, recognizing, acknowledging, and returning to the exercise, that your power of concentration and bare attention will gradually increase. In fact, the essence of these mindfulness exercises is really this process of repeatedly awakening and returning to the exercise. The exercises themselves serve mainly to give you something to grab onto—something to focus your attention on, and something to return to when your attention drifts. With time and practice, your ability to remain attentive, moment-to-moment, will increase dramatically, and the real power of mindfulness will become more and more evident.

Physical Discomfort

Physical discomfort while practicing these exercises, especially in a seated position, is inevitable. You will have aches in the back, knees, hips, neck, shoulders, and elsewhere. Your feet may fall asleep, you will have itches, muscle cramps, fatigue, shortness of breath, and so on. The urge to get up, change position, do something else, or stop altogether is difficult to resist at first.

The trick is to consciously recognize the discomfort, along with the urge to react to it, and to *refrain* from reacting immediately. Give yourself some time to step back, separate yourself from the discomfort, and observe the discomfort, along with the urge to react, without being controlled by it. Often, if you stay with it long enough, you will find the discomfort subsides on its own. If it does not, you can then go ahead and adjust your position as necessary.

Mental Discomfort

In practicing to develop mindfulness, you apply bare attention to what *is*, in the present moment, deliberately choosing to avoid distraction and external stimulation. In doing this you come face to face with yourself, your fears, your image of who and what you are, as well as your perception of your situation and condition in life. You must face yourself honestly and completely—the good, the bad and the ugly. For many of us, with the barrage of thoughts, feelings and emotions (the mental noise) that we encounter, this can be rather uncomfortable, if not downright unbearable.

The trick is to resolve to allow it all to be "O.K." Take that "step back," consciously recognizing that these thoughts and feelings are not *you*—they do not define you—they are just *thoughts* and *feelings*. Accept them without judgement, and, instead of giving in to the urge toward distraction, simply observe and identify that urge. Try to let the discomfort become just another part of the present moment experience to be observed, and then return to the exercise being practiced. Over time you will begin to see how judgement, fear and beliefs contribute to these thoughts and feelings. With practice the discomfort will subside and be overshadowed by the increasing insight and clarity that will be evident. Persistence is the key.

Boredom

The primary way that we practice mindfulness is by paying close attention to what is going on, during times when there is not much going on. At times you may feel that this practice is pointless, boring, a waste of time—that "there is more to life than *this*." It is inevitable that you will ask yourself, from time to time, "What am I doing this for? What is the point of this?" After all, we all have complicated and demanding lives that involve much more than what would be happening during those moments that we are practicing. You may feel that practice time would be better spent thinking about, or somehow addressing, other aspects of your life that you feel need attention.

Naturally, if there are things that urgently need to be done, it may be best to *mindfully* go about getting them done. But if you have set aside time for practicing mindfulness, by all means resist the notion that the time would be better spent doing something else. Remind yourself that you are practicing present moment awareness because the present moment is where your life takes place—to be effective in life you must *be* here, in the present moment. Remember that mindfulness is a skill, which, like any other, can only be developed through practice. Consciously recognize, "boredom is present," and return to the exercise being practiced. With persistence you will come to recognize mindfulness practice as one of your most important endeavors.

More on Labeling

As your practice strengthens, you will see with increasing clarity what is actually going on in your mind. As this happens you can begin labeling what you see. Labeling amounts to consciously recognizing and identifying what is happening in your mind. Labeling helps you maintain control of your present moment experience, and let go of distractions. It also increases your awareness of what is going on in your life that may need attention. I suggest you practice labeling your *thoughts* and your *mental state*. Though it is sometimes difficult to distinguish between thoughts and mental state, in general I would differentiate them as follows:

Labeling Thoughts: Here you recognize and label your actual thoughts in the moment. Some examples are: worrying, daydreaming, fantasizing, regretting, planning, anticipating or rehearsing the future, rehashing the past, "self-raising" (my term for thinking disparaging thoughts about others, trying to elevate your low self-image), "self-lowering" (my term for thinking disparaging thoughts about yourself, affirming your low self-image), "rambling" (when your thoughts ramble out of control), judging, analyzing, and there are countless more. Example: When you realize you are worrying, consciously recognize "worrying." When you realize you are self-raising, consciously recognize "self-raising."

Labeling Mental State: Here you recognize and label the general tone or underlying quality of your thoughts and feelings in the moment. Some examples of specific mental states are: fear, anger, joy, confusion, excitement, jubilation, apathy, hopelessness, confidence, certainty, exasperation, and there are countless more. Example: When you realize you are fearful, consciously recognize "fearful state of mind," or "fear is present," or just "fear." When you realize you are angry, consciously recognize "angry state of mind," or "anger is present," or just "anger."

Selfing

Practicing labeling your thoughts will be very enlightening. As your awareness increases you may be surprised to realize how much time you spend thinking about your "self." Most of us spend an enormous amount of time thinking about what we want, what we don't want, what we have and don't have, who we are, who we think we should be, what we could have been, what we believe, what we fear, where we are, where we wish we were, wondering why things aren't better for us, and on and on. Since this thinking activity is centered completely on the "self", I label it *"selfing."* "Selfing" is almost *constant* in many of us. As you develop mindfulness you will be struck by how much time you spend "selfing."

Mindfulness practice is the only thing that can save you from this curse. Your increasing awareness will eventually reveal the true nature of these "selfing" thoughts—they are utterly empty, boring, and without value. As this becomes more and more evident, "selfing" will begin to diminish.

On-going Practice

Following are several suggestions for how mindfulness can be practiced throughout the day. The object is to apply bare attention to

VITAL SKILL

what is going on in the moment, in the very midst of everyday pleasures, challenges, victories, failures, hassles, stress, confusion, boredom, etc. In on-going practice, as with dedicated practice, the breath serves as the *anchor* and *tether* to the present moment. Even while involved in other activities, it is possible to maintain a loose, "background" awareness of the breath. No matter where you are, or what you are doing, you can always ground yourself in the present moment by tuning into your breathing.

No matter how busy you are, it is possible to fit some of these exercises into your day. It just has to be made a priority. If you feel that you are so super-busy that you could not possibly fit mindfulness practice into your day, then you will probably burnout before long, if you keep doing what you are doing.

While the following techniques are quite simple and easy, the challenge lies in establishing the habit of *applying* them throughout your busy and hectic day. They have a three-step structure that takes a little time, but is very helpful for getting started. This three-step structure can be dropped after your practice has strengthened. The purpose of these exercises is to help keep you *"awake and attentive"* to the present moment experience throughout the day. They can be practiced *anywhere, anytime*.

6. <u>Pause, Breathe, Recognize</u>:

Pause: Normally, throughout the day, there are many things going through your mind. When you "pause," you *awaken* from the thoughts and distractions occupying your mind, and redirect your attention to what you are doing, and what is actually happening in and around you, in the present moment.

Breathe: Immediately upon pausing, tune into your breath, using exercise #2, "Following the Breath," as previously described. Breathe consciously for at least two or three breaths. If you become aware of tension in the abdomen, or anywhere in your body, consciously recognize and release it.

Recognize: This is a good exercise, especially for beginners, because the first three steps that follow, labeled "optional," reaffirm

VITAL SKILL

some of the basic principles presented in this book. To practice, take a moment to consciously recognize and comprehend the following:

"This is it." (optional) This is your life! Recognize that your life consists of whatever is happening right here and now. Realize that the very best you can do in this moment, to be your most effective, is to be awake and attentive to what is happening right here and now.

"No risk." (optional) Recognize that there is no risk to being in the present moment. There is nothing that is more important or urgent, and nothing you must first figure out, or plan. *You can trust the present moment.* It is safe to return to the present moment right now, without delay.

"The answers are here." (optional) Recognize that any answers, ideas, or solutions you need are available through present moment awareness (presence of mind)— worrying and thinking (mental noise) do not help. Recall that most of the worrying and thinking that we do is of no value.

Finally (this is the main step of the exercise), take a moment to recognize where you are, what you are doing, why you are doing it, and what's going on around you.

Try to keep your attention on the present moment experience, maintaining "background" awareness of the breath if possible.

7. <u>Pause, Breathe, Recall:</u>
Pause, Breathe: Perform these steps as previously described.
Recall: Take a moment to recognize and label, in retrospect, what thoughts, feelings, and/or mental state, you were experiencing just *before* pausing for this exercise.
Return your attention to the activity at hand, maintaining "background" awareness of the breath if possible.

8. Pause, Breathe, Experience:
Pause, Breathe: Perform these steps as previously described.
Experience: Take a moment to *experience* what is happening in the moment by tuning in to the six senses (touch, taste, smell, sight, sound, & mind). Are you hot or cold? What is touching your body? Are you hungry or thirsty? Is the wind blowing? Notice what sights and sounds are present. Are you feeling sad, happy, or anxious? Take a moment to *experience* what is happening.

Return your attention to the activity at hand, maintaining "background" awareness of the breath if possible.

9. Pause, Breathe, Release:
Pause, Breathe: Perform these steps as previously described.
Release: We all have our own "tension areas"—areas of the body where we unconsciously and habitually hold unnecessary muscular tension. Sometimes it can be hard to recognize these tension areas because we are so used to them. Some common tension areas are the face, scalp, neck, shoulders, abdomen, eyes, and groin. In this exercise, the focus is on consciously recognizing and releasing tension that you are holding in your body. Spend a moment to scan your body, from head to toe, to locate where you are holding tension (after a while you will identify several areas that are *always* tensed-up). Practice by consciously releasing the tension, for a period of at least a few breaths, in one or more of these areas. As you release tension, consciously recognize, "releasing." Remain conscious of the breath, and notice any feelings that arise.

Return your attention to the activity at hand, maintaining "background" awareness of the breath if possible.

10. Pause, Breathe, Posture:
Pause, Breathe: Perform these steps as previously described.
Posture: Take a moment to notice your bodily posture. Are you standing, sitting or lying down? What's happening with your spine (neck, upper and lower back), pelvis, and shoulders? What message is your posture sending to the world about you and your mental state?

VITAL SKILL

Are you projecting confidence, or hopelessness? Strength, or weakness? Remain conscious of the breath, and notice any feelings that arise.

Return your attention to the activity at hand, maintaining "background" awareness of the breath if possible.

11. Pause, Breathe, Smile:

Pause, Breathe: Perform these steps as previously described.

Smile: This is a very important exercise that has immediate benefit whenever practiced, anywhere, anytime. To practice, release all tension in your facial muscles, and allow your face to take on a hint of a smile (not a big grin, just a hint of a smile). Think of it as smiling to yourself, as you might when feeling a great sense of contentment and satisfaction. Notice how that sense of contentment and satisfaction becomes real. As you practice, consciously recognize, "releasing, smiling." Remain conscious of the breath, and notice any feelings that arise.

Return your attention to the activity at hand, maintaining "background" awareness of the breath if possible.

Practice Triggers

The above exercises are helpful only if practiced regularly and consistently every day, throughout the day. They should be practiced, ideally, whenever it occurs to you to practice them. In addition, I suggest identifying a few common, everyday events that occur regularly, and using these events as *"practice triggers,"* to remind you to do these exercises.

The idea is to develop the habit of practicing the exercises every time one of your "trigger" events occurs. Triggers are essential for starting out, to help you establish a consistent on-going practice. Some ideas for practice triggers are: entering the car, exiting the car, reaching for the radio (in the car), waiting at a stop light, reaching for the TV remote control, during TV commercials, picking up something to read, walking to the printer or copy machine, saving a file on the computer, sending a "print" command on the computer, pouring a cup of coffee, sipping a cup of coffee, starting a computer game, logging onto the internet, hearing the phone ring, hanging up the phone, changing a diaper, playing with children, hearing a child crying, feeling exasperated or stressed, whenever you handle your wallet or keys, or *any* event that occurs regularly and can be used to remind you to practice these mindfulness exercises. The possibilities are endless.

Mindfulness of Activity

Daily, routine activities are excellent vehicles for practicing mindfulness. Each day you perform countless activities that have become so routine that your attention is hardly required in order to perform them adequately. Some examples are: washing dishes, getting dressed, taking a shower, preparing food, speaking, walking, exercising, brushing teeth, lifting objects, sweeping the floor, unlocking the car door, doing laundry, making photo-copies—there are endless possibilities. The idea here is to select a few of these daily activities, and commit to doing them *mindfully*—consciously and deliberately—whenever you do them. Following are two specific methods you can use to practice mindfulness of activity:

12. Labeling: This technique makes use of the fact that any activity consists of a series of separate actions that are executed in succession. The practice consists of consciously recognizing and labeling the individual actions that comprise the activity, as you perform the activity. In most cases, practicing this exercise, it is beneficial to perform the activity more slowly and deliberately than normal; but it is up to you how slowly you practice, and how minutely you break the activity down into separate actions.

Example: While walking at a normal speed, you could practice mindfulness of activity by consciously recognizing and labeling each step: e.g. "stepping right," "stepping left," "stepping right," and so on. However, if you slowed the pace way down, the process of walking could be observed in much greater detail. You could break apart each step into three separate actions—lifting the foot off the ground, carrying it forward, and placing the foot back on the ground—practicing as follows: "lifting foot," "carrying foot," "placing foot," (other side) "lifting," "carrying," "placing," (other side) "lifting," "carrying," "placing."

Generally, the more slowly the activity is performed, and the more separate, distinct actions that are identified and labeled, the more powerful the technique. Some forethought and experimentation will help in determining what activities to use for this practice, and what separate actions to identify and label.

13. Visualizing: "Visualizing" is another way of practicing mindfulness of activity. This technique is practiced by *visualizing* the actions being executed, as they are executed. You actually create a mental image of what you are doing (the action you are executing), *as you are doing it*. It is not necessary to consciously construct the image to be visualized—once you establish the intention to visualize your actions, the mind will naturally form an image of whatever action or movement your attention is focused on in the moment. Accept whatever image the mind produces. You will find, with practice, that the mental image you form of what you are *doing* in the moment naturally merges with a mental image of what you are *intending* to do in that moment. The result is a sense of competence and precision in your actions, and the experience of absorption in the activity being performed.

Try this: You can get a sense of this technique with the following exercise: Close your eyes and visualize your right hand. *Slowly* clench and unclench your right hand repeatedly, visualizing your hand clenching and unclenching as you do it. Try to hold a clear image of your hand going through these motions, as it is happening. Try it with your left hand, and with both hands. Try it with different, more complex motions of the hands. Practice in this way until it is fairly easy to maintain a clear visualization, or image, of what your hands are doing. From that point, try applying this technique to other

VITAL SKILL

activities, such as walking, exercising, and household work. I use this technique all the time to practice mindfulness while walking, doing dishes, getting dressed, and many other times throughout the day.

Exercises for Effective Spoken Communication

Mindfulness lies at the heart of effective spoken communication. The ability to communicate effectively, one-to-one, is a wonderful skill for anyone to have, and is absolutely essential in many professions. We can consider spoken communication to consist of two components—*transmitting* and *receiving*:

Transmitting is your own *speaking*, plus all non-verbal messages and information you project.

Receiving is your own *listening,* plus reception of non-verbal messages and information that the other person is projecting.

If you can train yourself to be fully awake and attentive to the present moment experience *while* you are speaking (transmitting), and *while* you are listening (receiving), your ability to communicate effectively will dramatically improve.

The following two exercises provide a way of practicing mindfulness while speaking, and while listening. While they are challenging, and require focused concentration, they can be practiced as you go about your normal daily conversations, without any interruption or inconvenience. The real trick is *remembering* to practice these exercises. Your concentration will improve with practice, and you will find your ability to communicate effectively is greatly enhanced.

14. Mindfulness While Speaking: Have you had the experience of hearing yourself speak on tape, and thinking to yourself: "Do I really talk like that?" Speaking offers an excellent opportunity to practice mindfulness. Mindfulness of speaking helps you to speak clearly, and choose words that convey your ideas most effectively. With mindfulness you are more likely to refrain from speaking until your message is clearly formulated. Mindfulness is essential for effective spoken communication.

Technique: To speak mindfully it is first necessary to know what you want to say—the message you want to communicate must be clearly established in your mind. Mindfulness while speaking can then be practiced simply by *listening* to yourself speak, as you are speaking. You actually focus on *listening* to the words you are saying, as you say them. You can practice this exercise anytime you are conversing with someone, as well as when you are alone. For example, a good way to practice alone is to count to 100 out loud, focusing on listening to yourself as you count.

This technique provides a way to practice *focusing* your attention, or "tuning in," to what you are saying. Practicing this way, you are *aware* of the words you are saying—how they sound, what they mean, their pace, inflection, rhythm, volume, etc. You are aware of what you sound like, and the actual message contained in your words. You are actually hearing what your listeners are hearing. Knowing the message that you *intend* to convey, you gain a sense of how effectively you are communicating your intended message. This awareness, in turn, naturally enhances appropriate word selection as you continue speaking. Practicing this technique also helps you be more aware of the non-verbal messages your are sending as you speak. You will notice a dramatic improvement in your ability to speak effectively if you practice mindfulness while speaking.

15.   Mindfulness While Listening: Have you ever found yourself in a conversation, thinking about what you want to say next, or daydreaming about something, and completely missing what the other person is saying to you. Perhaps a client, colleague, or loved one is speaking to you, providing information that would be useful to you, and you have no idea what they have said. This happens to most of us on a fairly regular basis.   Effective communication requires that we pay attention—i.e. *listen*—when being spoken to.

Technique: Mindfulness while listening can be practiced by focusing on consciously and distinctly recognizing each word a person says as they are speaking. You could think of it as *"mentally saying,"*

VITAL SKILL

or *"thinking"* the words that the person is saying to you, as they say them. With practice, as your concentration improves, you will find that your mind is so quick, you can recognize the words that the person is saying, almost simultaneously, as the person says them. It will seem as though you are mentally saying, or thinking the words right along with the person.

This technique provides a way to practice *focusing* your attention, or "tuning in," to what the other person is saying as they speak. It is impossible for your mind to wander while engaged in this technique. With practice you will find that you not only catch every word that is said, but also the more subtle non-verbal messages and information that always accompany spoken communication. You can even practice this alone, while listening to the radio or TV.

16. <u>Walking Meditation:</u> Walking deserves special mention because it is such a good trigger event to remind you to practice mindfulnesss. You can use one of the following three practice techniques anytime you are walking:

Exercise #12, "Labeling", is a good method. Using this technique to practice walking meditation is covered in the general description of that exercise.

Exercise #13, "Visualizing", is another good method. When walking, visualize any aspect of the activity. For example, as you walk you could visualize the movement of your legs and/or feet, your overall posture, or the movements of you arms. What *specifically* you focus on is not that important, as long as it has to do the the activity of walking.

The last walking exercise, which I practice often, is what I call "treading lightly". Here you focus on the actual placement of your feet on the ground as you walk. The idea is to practice placing your feet down as *lightly* as possible, to the extent you can without walking awkwardly. A good way to think of this exercise is that you are trying to walk in such a way as to minimize the wear-and-tear on the soles of your shoes. Be aware of any unnecessary tension in the feet or legs when you practice this. If you do a lot of walking, this exercise may save you a few dollars on shoe maintenance.

17.   Yoga Practice: Yoga practice makes up part of my personal mindfulness practice. I practice Hatha Yoga in the tradition of B.K.S. Iyengar. Very briefly, this involves practicing a series of bodily postures, called asanas (AH-sa-nas), with attention focused primarily on posture, precise body alignment, movement from one asana to the next, and breath. If approached as such, yoga is an excellent practice for the development of mindfulness. An added bonus of the Iyengar style (and many other styles as well) is that it is particularly vigorous, and is superb for the development of strength and flexibility. It is beyond the scope of this book to actually provide yoga instruction, but there are competent teachers in practically every metropolitan area, and I would encourage you to seek one out. Yoga is a good mindfulness practice, and it will help keep your body in peak condition.

Establishing a Daily Practice

I encourage you to establish a daily mindfulness practice, even a modest one, right away. Using a just a few of the exercises and techniques listed above, for both dedicated and on-going practice, make it a priority to practice these exercises on a daily basis. To get started you can follow these steps to design a daily practice:

1.   Establish a daily, dedicated practice by spending at least 5–10 minutes, preferably twice per day, practicing exercise #1 or #2—these are the best ones for starting out. Over time, (perhaps a few months) gradually increase the time to 20–30 minutes, and experiment with exercises #3–#5.

2.   Identify one or two events that happen frequently throughout the day, and designate them as "practice triggers" (see page 94). Develop the habit of practicing one of exercises #6–#11 whenever one

VITAL SKILL

of these trigger events occurs. Exercise #6 is a good one for starting out, but if any of the others are more appealing to you, then use them. <u>Important</u>: To begin with, I suggest that you select *just one* of the techniques and *stay with it*—it will be challenging enough to establish the habit of practicing without the complication of trying to remember multiple exercises. After you have established your practice you can begin experimenting with the other exercises and incorporate more trigger events. See Appendix B for more ideas on this.

3. Identify one or two activities that you perform on a daily basis, and commit to doing them mindfully from now on, using one of exercises #12 or #13. (see page 99) Again, choose one technique and stay with it until your practice is well established. After a while, try the other exercise from this group, and add to your list of activities. See Appendix B for more ideas on this.

After you feel you have settled into a regular daily practice, try the following:

4. Identify one or two people in your life, perhaps a spouse or colleague, and commit to practice *Mindfulness while Speaking and Listening* when communicating with these individuals.

5. Finally, practice *Mindfulness of Gratitude* and/or *Mindfulness of Love's Path* in all situations.

Following the above steps, and with conviction and commitment, you can establish a daily mindfulness practice with minimal change to your current daily routine.

<u>Resistance:</u>
There are many forms of resistance that you may encounter related to daily mindfulness practice. The most prominent for the newcomer is a lack of conviction that mindfulness can really have a

positive impact in his/her life. Others, like physical or mental discomfort, are discussed in an earlier section.

More subtle forms of resistance usually result from unconscious beliefs that create feelings of uneasiness at the prospect of practicing and living with mindfulness. You may find that while mindfulness seems to make sense generally, this resistance makes you feel that the effort to develop mindfulness may not be a good investment for you personally. And even if you have arrived at firm conviction and commitment to the effort of developing mindfulness, you may still experience resistance in actually getting started with the practice itself.

If you find that what is presented in this book makes sense, but feel resistant to it for some reason, then I suggest there may be some unconscious beliefs acting. I recommend the following exercise to help you see what beliefs, if any, are causing this resistance:

Sit down with a pencil and piece of paper. Spend a few minutes contemplating this whole business of mindfulness. Think about the effort that would be required, in the form of practice, to develop mindfulness. Think about how you might benefit from more highly developed mindfulness, and what it would be like to live your life mindfully. Then ask yourself the following questions, one at a time, writing down whatever answers come to mind:

1. What am I afraid might happen if I undertake the effort to develop mindfulness? Why do I think this would happen?
2. What am I afraid might happen if I live my life with my attention/awareness/consciousness anchored in the present moment? Why do I think this would happen?
3. What am I afraid might happen if I live my life with open acceptance of what exists in the present moment? Why do I think this would happen?

Examine what you have written down. The answers to these questions might point to unconscious beliefs that have you feeling hesitant.

VITAL SKILL

Part III

VITAL SKILL

Beyond Effectiveness

Of course effectiveness isn't *everything*. There must be something that lies beyond effectiveness. How about *Happiness*? What good is effectiveness if we aren't happy? The practice exercises in Part II are essential to develop mindfulness. But ultimately, we must take this amazing skill of mindfulness we have developed, go out into the world, and put it to use not only to be more effective, but also to be more *happy*.

The professional musician has spent hours upon hours, years upon years, practicing scales, fingering exercises, developing technique, learning pieces, to lay the foundation to be able to do what he does. But you don't go to a concert to hear someone play fingering exercises on stage. You go to hear someone play a piece of music, maybe by Bach or Mozart, with all their heart and soul. When the musician gets on stage to perform, he doesn't think about scales, fingerings, technique, etc.—those things have become a part of him, and are there to serve him. When he is on stage to perform, he moves beyond scales and exercises, and *plays music*. He uses all the skill he has developed to *play music*. He's not worrying about making mistakes, or what people in the crowd are thinking. He just *plays*.

Being happy is kind of like playing music. When you *choose* to be happy, you are like the musician who steps on stage and plays a piece of music with everything he's got. A piece of music doesn't just happen by itself—it is nothing but a bunch of symbols on paper until a musician transforms it into music. Happiness is the same way—it doesn't just happen by itself. Happiness by itself is just an idea. It doesn't really *exist* until someone steps up and *decides to be happy*. External circumstances can make that choice very easy, or very difficult, depending upon what is going on. But we should be very

VITAL SKILL

clear that happiness is *always* available to us and is *always* a choice that we make. Whether conscious or unconscious, it is our choice, or decision to be happy in the present moment that makes us happy.

Like the musician who has laid a solid foundation of technical and musical ability from which to work, we must also work from a solid foundation to be able to choose happiness at will, regardless of external circumstances. And you guessed it, mindfulness is that foundation. Happiness, like everything else, happens *one moment at a time, in the present moment*. The skill of mindfulness, as developed by the exercises of Part II, is *essential* for choosing happiness. Below, I describe three practices, *Present Moment Goals, Mindfulness of Gratitude* and *Mindfulness of Love's Path*, that will help you apply mindfulness to the important task of *choosing* happiness in the present moment.

I consider these techniques to be the ultimate mindfulness practice. Practicing these techniques, building upon the foundation created by the exercises of Part II, you employ the skill of mindfulness to radically transform your present moment experience. The power here lies in the fact that, as we have discussed, *your present moment experience constitutes your entire life. If you transform your present moment experience, you transform your entire life.* These practices are almost *medicinal* in their ability to help you maintain a positive outlook on life.

Present Moment Goals

You may wonder how mindfulness practice, with its emphasis on present moment awareness and acceptance of the present moment reality, will ever help you reach the goals you have set for the future. "If all I do is focus on what is happening right here and now, and accept everything as being just fine, how is anything ever going to change? How am I ever going to take control of my life, and make things happen to achieve my goals?"

VITAL SKILL

It's a good question. Mindfulness inherently requires a certain "letting go" of trying to control events and outcomes. Mindfulness does not lend itself to excessive planning of the future, worrying about the future, and all the efforts aimed at shaping the future that go along with trying to control life. So the question arises: "What is to keep everything from grinding to a halt? How will I keep my life *moving* in the direction I want it to go?"

We must first recognize that no matter what we do, we ultimately have very little, if any, direct control over life. Life pretty much just happens, in the form of our present moment experience. The only thing we can directly control is how we choose to *feel* and *respond* in the present moment. The interesting thing is, we find that how we choose to respond in the present moment plays a primary role in *shaping* our present moment experience. In other words, getting back to our time-line, how we respond in moment "a" influences our experience in moment "b." Over time we see that our life situation, the external circumstances we attract to ourselves, tends to *reflect* and *support* how we habitually choose to feel and respond in the present moment.

For example, if you habitually choose to see yourself as a victim in your present moment experience, you will find reasons within your experience to *feel* like a victim, and you will ultimately attract to yourself external circumstances that *appear* to make you a victim. If, on the other hand, you habitually choose to see yourself as very fortunate in your present moment experience, you will find reasons within your experience to *feel* very fortunate, and you will ultimately attract to yourself external circumstances that make you *appear* to be very fortunate.

Simply put, our present moment choices determine our present moment experience. If this is not apparent to you in your own life, it is because your choices are not *conscious*. If you are not conscious of your present moment choices, there is no way you could see their connection to your present moment experience.

Mindfulness enables us to choose *consciously*. When we choose *consciously* in the present moment, we find that we *do* have a sense of control over our life and life situation. But the key is, once again, that this sense of control is based entirely on our ability to consciously choose how we feel and respond in the present moment. This is where the vital skill of mindfulness comes into play.

We should also keep in mind The First Law of Change: *Change happens one moment at a time, in the present moment.* While we know that things *will* change in the future, we also know the when things *do* change, it will be the present moment. Change *happens* only in the present moment. Charting a detailed course into the future, then struggling to stay on that course is not the best way to go because all the things you plan to happen in the future cannot happen "*in the future*"—they can only happen here and now, in the present moment. The actions, initiatives, changes, answers, information, solutions, ideas, opportunities, lucky breaks, etc., that can help you move toward achieving your goals, can materialize only in the present moment. If your gaze is fixed a few miles ahead on the course you have charted into the future, you will miss the very gifts you are searching for because they can only be found right here, in the present moment.

Practicing *present moment goals* is a way that the skill of mindfulness can be used to help you move toward concrete *future goals* you want to achieve. When we think of goals, we usually think of future goals—goals that we hope to achieve at some time in the future. What distinguishes a present moment goal from a future goal is that *a present moment goal is a goal that can only be realized in the present moment.* A present moment goal can be thought of as a desired state of mind, a feeling, or an experience, which can be achieved in the present moment, and can *only* be achieved in the present moment. Practicing present moment goals is valuable because it will help you clarify and better understand your future goals, and give you a way to bring them closer to your present moment experience.

The best way to formulate present moment goals is to start with your future goals. Begin by closely examining the future goals you have set for yourself. Look deeply at these goals to discover *why* you want to achieve them. Why are they important to you? What do these goals really mean to you? How do you expect to *feel,* or what do you expect to *experience* when you have achieved your goals? If you do this, you will discover that every future goal has an *essence*—a *feeling* or *experience* that you expect to have when you actually achieve that goal. A future goal is simply the set of external circumstances you believe must be present in your life to create that desired feeling or experience, which I refer as the goal's *essence*. If you look closely enough, you will see that it was ultimately the attainment of this feeling or experience *alone* that attracted you to that future goal in the first place.

Future goals are based on the belief that something in your world, external to you, must change before the feeling or experience you desire is available to you. Present moment goals, on the other hand, are based on the belief that the feeling or experience you seek is really nothing more that a state of mind, which is available to you this very moment. With practice, you can gain the ability to create the desired feeling or experience without having to wait for external circumstances to change. You will find you can experience the essence of your future goals in the present moment, and, in doing so, help remove the obstacles to creating the external circumstances that would support that essence. In other words, practicing present moment goals will help you to achieve your future goals.

For example, suppose that you and I both have the same future goal of having a lot of money. Suppose we both decided that the best way to accomplish our goal was to find additional part-time work, and to begin attending night classes to try to improve our money earning prospects.

While we share exactly the same future goal, and the same approach to achieving our goal, the *essence* of that goal may be completely different for each of us. It could be that for you, the essence of having more money is that it signifies you are financially successful, and financial success is what makes you feel *worthy* as a person. The essence of your goal of having money is that you believe having money means you are worthy—you have real *worth*. On the other hand, for me, the essence of having more money might be that it alleviates a deep fear of becoming sick or disabled, and unable to earn a living as I get older. Having money means that I will be able to take care of myself as I get older, and that gives me a feeling of safety. The essence of my goal of having more money is that I believe having money means that I am *safe*.

If we took the time to examine our common future goal of having more money, and discovered the essence of that goal for each of us, we could then formulate *present moment goals* to practice. The present moment goal for you would be to cultivate, in the present moment, the feeling of having worth, or feeling worthy as a person. For me it would be to cultivate, in the present moment, the feeling of being safe—of knowing that I will be taken care of. These are both feelings that can be *practiced* and *realized* by each of us, in the present moment, without having any more money that we have right now. To practice this we might begin by using affirmations—positive statements affirming that we are, in this moment, *worthy*, or *safe* respectively. We would also work on creating the *feelings* of worth and safety in the present moment. With practice we would find that we can create those feelings at will.

The key is that in the process of trying to create these feelings of worth, or safety, we would inevitably encounter the specific unconscious beliefs that *cause* us to feel unworthy, or unsafe to begin with. There is no way we could approach the feelings of worth or safety without confronting these beliefs.

In practicing the present moment goal of feeling worthy, you would discover that you simply *believe* you are unworthy (remember, our core beliefs don't necessarily make sense). This could be the result, for example, of being told you were a "bad boy/girl" repeatedly throughout your early years, with the result that you eventually learned to feel unworthy. Here is a previously *unconscious* belief that has no real truth to it, but may have had tremendous influence precisely *because* it was unconscious. You want more money because you also believe that having a lot of money equates to having *worth* as a person.

But recall that we always strive, unconsciously, to create results that support and fulfill our beliefs. The catch is that with these two beliefs at work, you cannot allow yourself more money because having more money, with the resulting feeling of *worth*, would not support and fulfill your belief that you are inherently *unworthy*. The need to fulfill both of these beliefs—that you are inherently unworthy, and that money equates to worth—clearly forms an obstacle to you ever having substantially more money.

In practicing the present moment goal of feeling safe, I might discover that I believe it is unsafe to grow old; that sickness, disability, or somehow being unable to support one's self are inevitable aspects of growing older. This belief could be the result of repeatedly being told this as a child, perhaps by older people in my life who were disabled, broke, and unable to support themselves. This previously *unconscious* belief, again, has no real truth to it, but could be very influential precisely *because* it is unconscious. I want more money because I also believe that having more money will protect me from this fate (I must have been told this as well). I believe that more money will somehow keep me safe as I get older.

But as we know, I will strive unconsciously to create results that support and fulfill *both* of these beliefs. The catch for me is that having more money come to me, with the result of feeling *safe*, would be in direct conflict with my belief that it is *unsafe* to grow old. The beliefs that it is unsafe to get old, and that money will keep me safe as I age, together are clearly obstacles to my ever having more money in my life.

As we more clearly identify beliefs surrounding our present moment goals, we see that these same beliefs are often the principle obstacles to our achieving the *future* goals that we started with (in our example, the goal of having more money). No amount of part-time work and night classes would enable either of us to reach our goal of having more money until we had faced and dealt with these limiting beliefs. With awareness of our beliefs we have the opportunity to evaluate them, decide if they serve our best interest, and deal with them to remove the obstacles standing between our goals and us.

We should also note that the beliefs we discovered—your belief that you are *unworthy,* and my belief that I am *unsafe*—unconscious though they may be, amount to *choices* that we are making in the present moment. In this example you and I are unconsciously *choosing* to feel unworthy and unsafe, respectively, in our present moment experience. In order to bring more money into our lives we would need to come to this realization, dismantle these limiting beliefs, and *choose differently.* This is not possible without mindfulness.

To get started practicing present moment goals, I suggest you use the following technique which combines breath awareness with a positive affirming statement of your present moment goal. To practice your present moment goal of feeling *worthy*, you would practice as follows:

- Breathing in, consciously recognize: "Breathing in, I am present."
- Breathing out, consciously recognize: "Breathing out, I know I am worthy."
- Repeat indefinitely.

To practice my present moment goal of feeling *safe*, I would practice as follows:

- Breathing in, consciously recognize: "Breathing in, I am present."
- Breathing out, consciously recognize: "Breathing out, I know I am safe."
- Repeat indefinitely.

Mindfulness of Gratitude

Mindfulness of Gratitude is the conscious feeling of gratitude for some aspect of your present moment experience. It is the present moment awareness of the good, positive things in your life to be grateful for, along with the experience or *feeling* of gratitude.

"When we are happy, we are truly grateful. The reverse also holds true. When we are grateful, we are truly happy. In fact, oftentimes I call gratitude the sweetest way to embrace happiness. We can cut through all the misery by turning our attention to being grateful. In spite of all the catastrophes that might occur, we can find in little and big ways bottomless wellsprings for our thankfulness. Gratitude then becomes the shortest of shortcuts to happiness."

(from Barry Neil Kaufman, *Happiness is a Choice*, p.187)

Gratitude is the Essence of Receiving

You may have many good, wonderful things in your life, but these blessings exist for you only when you consciously *receive* them in the present moment. If you are not aware of them, do not appreciate them, or do not recognize their goodness, then they truly don't exist for you in that moment. Gratitude is the very essence of receiving. It is as if gratitude is an integral part of, or is contained *within* every blessing. It is always there, but you must learn to *tune-in* to it, or become *mindful* of that gratitude, in order for those blessings to be real to you.

Ultimately, if you want to experience more good things in the future, as we all do, it is essential to first learn the art of receiving the good things that are already here, in the present moment. This is accomplished with the practice of Mindfulness of Gratitude.

Practicing Gratitude

Practicing Mindfulness of Gratitude is very simple—you simply make gratitude your Present Moment Goal. Pause, breathe, and smile (see exercise #11), then *choose* to be grateful—choose to feel gratitude for your present moment experience. Consciously direct your attention to the task of creating, or giving rise to the feeling of gratitude. When getting started, you may need to deliberately find something in your present moment experience to feel grateful for. Or, put another way, you may need to find a *reason* to feel grateful for your present moment experience. This may be difficult and require some thought at first, especially in challenging or undesirable situations. If it is difficult to create the actual *feeling* of gratitude, you can start by mentally

VITAL SKILL

repeating a simple *statement* of gratitude. With practice, finding reasons to be grateful, and creating the feeling of gratitude will become much easier. The important thing is to practice making the conscious choice, and effort, to recognize and feel a sense of gratitude for some aspect of what is happening in the present moment. And don't forget to smile!

It is always possible, no matter what the present moment experience is, to find some reason to feel grateful. Difficult and painful experiences always contain valuable life lessons. Opportunities to grow and learn surround us constantly, and no matter how bad things are, they could always be worse. Ultimately, you will find it is always appropriate to be grateful, no matter what the present moment holds.

My favorite gratitude practice is to feel grateful for present moment awareness:

> Upon awakening to the present moment, I feel very grateful for having awakened to the opportunity to practice mindfulness. If you think about it, it is a *huge* blessing to awaken to the present moment and have the opportunity to be mindful. It is like being brought back to life—like being rescued from oblivion. The present moment is your only chance to be fully alive and awake, and to make real contact with the world. The moment you return to the present moment, the sensations of wakefulness, clarity, calm, and stability are immediately felt. It is truly a blessing.

You can practice as follows:
- Pause, Breathe, and Smile (Exercise #11)
- Breathing in: "Breathing in, I am present."
- Breathing out: "Breathing out, I am grateful."
- Repeat indefinitely.

If you have difficulty finding something to feel grateful for, here are some ideas. Feel grateful for:

- Having awakened to the opportunity to practice Mindfulness of Gratitude.
- Not having a toothache. (If you have ever had a bad toothache, you know how *magnificent* it is not to have one!)
- Having food, shelter, clothing.
- Present moment awareness.
- Witnessing an act of kindness.
- A cool breeze.
- Warm sunshine.
- The miracle of life.
- There are endless possibilities.

Mindfulness of Love's Path

Love has many attributes that we would all do well to emulate. Among those attributes, I would include the following:

- Love is always present.
- Love trusts and embraces what is.
- Love is patient.
- Love is fearless.
- Love knows only abundance.
- Love is supremely confident.
- Love is always happy.
- Love never judges.
- Love regrets nothing.
- Love knows no guilt.
- Love never worries.
- Love is ever optimistic.
- Love doesn't try to control things.
- Love acts for the benefit of all.
- Love is always truthful.
- Love is generous and kind.
- Love is ever grateful.

- Love cannot be harmed, and can do no harm.

Being mindful of Love's Path means being able to receive Love's guidance. It means being able, if for just a moment, to take on even one of the above attributes, make it your own, and see where it would lead you. Using the above list, or your own list, take some time to contemplate Love's attributes, and what it would mean for you to "make them your own."

Practicing Mindfulness of Love's Path is very simple. You can be mindful of Love's Path, in the present moment, by simply asking yourself "What would Love do here?" This simple question, "What would Love do here?", is magical when you truly seek an answer. But sincerity is the key here - you must be sincere in your asking, you must truly want to see Love's Path, or nothing really happens. When you seek the answer to this question you find the following:

- Your mind becomes quiet. You return to the present moment, and whatever mental noise may have been present—worry, anger, confusion—fades away. It is impossible to receive the answer to this question unless your mind is very quiet. Mindfulness practice gives you the power to quiet your mind with ease.

- With a quiet mind, the answer is there, without fail. Love's Path, in that moment, is crystal clear.

- Love's Path is always very simple and easy to follow. It usually amounts to nothing more than a shift in perception—the simple choice to smile, accept the present moment experience without judgement, and feel happy or grateful, leaving you free to pursue your heart's desires and life purpose without reservation.

Do not concern yourself with *following* Love's Path, at least not at first. The point here is just to sense it, to be aware, or mindful of it.

VITAL SKILL

Practice by asking yourself "What would love do here?" throughout the day. You might set aside a day or two each week and make this your practice for the day. You will find it is a very powerful technique for countering negativity—whether it is anger, fear, sorrow, hurt, or whatever, Mindfulness of Love's Path will help you rise above it. The sense of peaceful acceptance that results from this practice is immediately felt.

You can get a sense of this by doing the following exercise:

Take a few moments to contemplate Love's attributes as listed above. Then think about an event or situation in your life that is very stressful. Whether it is being reprimanded by your boss at work, or facing three fussy children at home, use your imagination to *place* yourself in a stressful situation you are familiar with. *Feel* the anger, humiliation, frustration, or whatever feeling you experience in this situation. Then ask yourself; "What would Love do here?" Hold the image of that stressful situation in mind, breathe, smile, and ask again; "What would Love do here?" Stay with it for a moment and see if Mindfulness of Love's Path offers a new way to respond in this situation.

When you actually find yourself in one of these stressful situations try practicing as follows:

- Pause, Breathe, and Smile (Exercise #11)
- Breathing in: "Breathing in, I am here."
- Breathing out: "Breathing out, what would love do here?"
- Repeat.

No Self

Perhaps the most fundamental of Love's attributes is that Love has no "self," or "ego" that must be protected, defended, justified, validated, compensated, recognized, bolstered, coddled, vindicated, respected, admired, made to feel special, etc.

Your "self," or "ego" arisis when you identify with your *mind's* definition of who you are. Your mind creates and defines your "self" so as to distinguish *you,* from all else in the world. Mind accomplishes this by producing an endless stream of thoughts that focus on *you*—what you want, what you have, what you wish you were, what you think others think you should be, what you look like, what you want to look like, etc. In fact, most of the "mental noise" we discussed earlier is simply your mind working hard to maintain, affirm, and strengthen its image of your "self," as distinct from everything else. You will find that following Love's Path ultimately requires detaching from, or letting go of mind's image of "self." When you are able to do this you will be *amazed* at how much simpler and lighter life is, without the need to maintain and protect that complex, burdensome mental creation—your "*self.*"

Your physical nature creates a convincing *appearance* of separateness and distinctness, and this makes it very difficult to eliminate the concept of "self." But eliminating the concept of "self" is not really necessary. The trick is being mindful that your sense of self is just a concept, or an idea. Recognize "self" for what it is: it is an illusion, a product of your mind that consists of nothing more than mind's incessant self-oriented thoughts. The "self" is not *real*. The truth of this can only be seen by dismantling mind's *wall* of self-oriented thinking, and getting a glimpse of what is behind it. This is possible through mindfulness. With mindfulness practice the self-oriented thinking, i.e. mental noise, begins to subside, and the real nature of "self" becomes more and more apparent.

A good way to gain the proper perspective on this is to think of your "self" as being transparent and massless, or without matter. As an exercise, try to imagine your body to be this way—transparent and massless. Try thinking of your body as being an energy field, rather than a solid, massive structure. With this image you get a more realistic view of the "self"—it is here, but it has no substance, no reality. With this exercise you can also sense that with no "self," there is no resistance, no pain, no judgment, no vulnerability, no fear.

The "self" *craves* substance and it *craves* to be real, but its craving can never be satisfied. Mind will try every trick in the book—it will struggle endlessly to make you *believe* that your "self" is not only real and substantial, but that it is the very center of your existence. Without a high degree of mindfulness your life is controlled almost *completely* by your mind's efforts to assert the "self." But the "self" does not have, and never will have substance and reality. You must dismantle mind's wall of self-oriented thinking and detach from your "self," in order to follow Love's Path.

VITAL SKILL

Conclusion

This is it! This moment—the never-ending, ever-changing present moment—is all there is. Success, fulfillment, and happiness cannot be found in the past; they cannot be found in the future; they can only be found right here, right now, in the present moment.

Mindfulness is a *vital* skill. It is vital in the sense that it is essential to life; it manifests life; it is full of life and vigor. It is the only way we can ever come to clearly see and understand who we are, our heart's desire and life purpose, and all that is happening in us and around us. Mindfulness enables us to be fully alive.

Mindfulness is also the foundation of true effectiveness. Effectiveness is very important. True effectiveness leads us toward success and fulfillment and is relevant in every aspect of life.

Ultimately it comes down to a simple choice: to be here now, where your life is taking place, or not. Choose mindfulness. Choose to be here. Undertake mindfulness practice, stay with it, and you will reach a point of no return, where there is no turning back. You will come to know the sense of wakefulness, clarity, calm, and stability that mindfulness produces. Eventually you will feel so completely at home and secure in present moment awareness that you will wonder how you ever got along as your former, "pre-mindfulness" self. At that point mindfulness practice will be an important part of your life that you could not imagine giving up.

VITAL SKILL

Appendix A: Summary of Important Points

1. *Mindfulness* is the skill of being fully awake and attentive to the present moment experience. With this definition, there are three main points:

   - Mindfulness is a skill, which, like any other skill, requires *conviction, commitment*, and most of all, *practice*. Practice is the ultimate key.
   - Mindfulness means paying attention, on a consistent and sustained basis, to the present moment experience.
   - Mindfulness requires openly accepting the present moment reality, just as it is.

2. *True Effectiveness* is the ability to produce a definite and desired result, which contributes to your experience of success and fulfillment in life. "Success" and "fulfillment" are entirely a function of your individual heart's desire and life purpose.

3. Mindfulness and Effectiveness are connected through The First Law of Effectiveness: *Effectiveness happens one moment at a time, in the present moment.*

4. The First Law of Life: *Life happens one moment at a time, in the present moment.*

5. Present Moment Orientation: Conscious awareness that life—all that happens, all that is—is contained entirely within the present moment. There is nothing other than what is here and now. *This is it!*

VITAL SKILL

6. We can distinguish between your "life situation" and your "life." Your "life situation" is the circumstance, or situation in which you find yourself. It consists of your occupation, relationships, past experience, future prospects, financial status, and all else that is external to you. But your *"life"* is independent of your past, future, or anything external. Your "life" consists of nothing other than your actual present moment experience.

7. The essence and building block of mindfulness is *bare attention*—focused and sustained attention to the present moment experience without judgement, analysis, or concern for results or benefits. The power of mindfulness arises from bare attention.

8. Unconscious thinking—"mental noise"—has no substance, and is of no value.

9. Effectiveness is made real by your interactions with the world, and your *beliefs* are at the core of determining how you interact with the world. Mindfulness is the only way to see clearly how your unconscious beliefs influence your interactions. This awareness is essential to effectively deal with limiting beliefs.

10. Fear can work in a million ways to hinder your effectiveness. Mindfulness is the only way to see clearly how fear is operating in your life. This awareness is essential to effectively manage fear.

11. Planning and worrying do not help you control your future. Remember that the future consists of nothing but present moments that have yet to happen. To take care of the future, you must take care of the present moment. *The present moment is your future—they are one and the same.* The only way you can have any sense of control over your future is to have a sense of control over your present moment experience. You can do this by *consciously* choosing your response to the present moment experience. Mindfulness is the key.

VITAL SKILL

12. Open, happy acceptance of the present moment reality, including conditions and situations you don't like, is crucial. Dissatisfaction, discontentment, and worry are not helpful. Present moment awareness of your heart's desire and life purpose (clear recollection) is the best motivator you have for working toward positive change.

13. The consequences of your actions, choices and decisions cannot be avoided. All actions, choices, and decisions happen one moment at a time, in the present moment. To manage the consequences you face, you must manage your actions, choices, and decisions in the present moment. This requires mindfulness.

14. The key to dealing effectively with stress lies in consciously *responding* to stressors, rather than unconsciously and automatically *reacting* to stressors. This takes mindfulness. Mindfulness enables you to see when stress reactivity is kicking in, and to consciously choose differently—to *not* allow your automatic and unconscious reactions to take over.

15. Mindfulness practice gives rise to the following three faculties that form the foundation of true effectiveness:

    - Clear perception: The ability to perceive the true nature of what is going on, inside and outside yourself, in the present moment.
    - Clear Recollection: A clear, present moment awareness of your heart's desire and life purpose in relation to the goals, aspirations, and intentions that drive your efforts.
    - Presence of Mind: Being *right here, right now*, with your attention, awareness, and consciousness in the present moment, where all your actions, choices, and decisions take place.

16. Mindfulness is at the heart of effective spoken communication. To speak and listen effectively, there is no substitute for the ability to

VITAL SKILL

"tune in," and apply focused attention to what your are saying, or what is being said.

17. Mindfulness of Gratitude and Mindfulness of Love's Path are the ultimate mindfulness practices. They are powerful ways you can employ the skill of mindfulness to truly transform your present moment experience, and thus your entire life.

18. The key is to establish a daily practice. Without a daily mindfulness practice, this book is nothing more than a bunch of words on paper. Follow the steps beginning on page 100 to get started.

Appendix B: "80 Ways" to Be More Mindful

The following table lists 80 different common activities and events, and indicates some exercises that are good matches for each activity or event. These are a few suggestions only—there are infinite possibilities. It is provided to help you broaden your thinking on how the exercises in this book can be incorporated into your day. Feel free to alter or expand this list.

EVENTS / ACTIVITIES	EXERCISES														
At home:	1	2	3	4	5	6	7	8	9	10	11	12	13	14	15
Waking in the morning.						x			x		x				
Getting out of bed.													x		
Going to sleep	x	x	x	x	x	x									
Walking up/down stairs.		x								x			x		
Exercising/stretching.										x			x		
Dedicated practice.	x	x	x	x	x										
Preparing food.						x					x		x		
Eating food.						x		x				x	x		
Taking a shower.							x	x	x			x	x		
Getting dressed.									x				x		
Greeting a family member.						x					x			x	x
Speaking to a family member.						x					x			x	x
Disciplining a child.		x				x								x	x
Playing with a child.						x					x			x	x
Dealing with an upset child.		x				x								x	x

127

VITAL SKILL

Turning on the TV.						x				x				
Watching TV.		x				x		x	x	x					x
Reaching for TV the remote.						x				x				
Washing dishes.								x		x	x			
Doing laundry.										x	x			
Ironing clothes.								x		x	x			
Sweeping the floor.								x		x	x			
Cutting the grass.										x	x			
Raking leaves.										x	x			
Gardening.		x				x		x			x			
General, throughout day.	1	2	3	4	5	6	7	8	9	10	11	12	13	14	15
Walking, anytime.		x				x	x			x			x		
Handling keys.						x							x		
Handling wallet.						x							x		
Speaking.														x	
Standing, waiting.		x				x	x		x	x	x				
Sitting, waiting.		x				x	x		x	x	x				
Getting in/out of car.		.											x		
Warming up the car.						x	x	x	x						
Driving a car.		x				x			x	x			x		
Reaching for the car radio.						x							x		
Sitting at a stop light.		x					x		x						
Riding the bus or subway.		x				x	x		x		x				
Feeling any strong emotion.		x					x	x	x		x				
In the office:	1	2	3	4	5	6	7	8	9	10	11	12	13	14	15
Sitting at desk.		x				x	x		x						
Pouring a cup of coffee.						x							x		
Drinking a cup of coffee.							x	x							
Walking to copier or fax.		x								x	x		x		

VITAL SKILL

Making copies.									x	x					
Sending a fax.								x		x					
Turning on computer.				x								x			
Logging onto internet.				x				x							
Sending a print command.				x				x	x						
Before picking up phone.									x						
Speaking on phone.													x		
Hanging up phone.							x			x					
Start of a meeting.		x			x			x	x						x
Speaking to boss.								x					x	x	
Speaking to co-worker.													x	x	
Speaking to customer.								x					x	x	
Feeling bored.		x				x	x	x							
Feeling stressed.		x			x	x	x	x	x	x					
Feeling frustrated.		x			x		x	x		x					
Feeling intimidated.		x			x		x	x		x					
Recreation / Leisure	1	2	3	4	5	6	7	8	9	10	11	12	13	14	15
Playing golf.		x				x			x				x	x	
Playing tennis.													x		
Playing any sport.									x				x		
Hiking or climbing.		x											x		
Fishing.										x			x		
Handling a fish.						x									
Sun bathing.		x				x	x	x		x					
Dancing.							x						x		
Playing music.							x						x		
Painting or drawing.													x		
Looking at a menu.						x				x					
Having a drink.		x				x		x		x					

VITAL SKILL

Manual Work	1	2	3	4	5	6	7	8	9	10	11	12	13	14	15
Lifting a heavy object.													x		
Handling fragile materials.													x		
Handling hazardous materials.													x		
Counting / sorting items.													x		
Using power tools.						x							x		
Using sharp tools.						x							x		
Hammering a nail.						x							x		
Tightening a screw.						x							x		
Digging.						x							x		
House painting.						x							x		
Working on a ladder.						x							x		

Appendix C: Sources

The following references were quoted in this book.

1. DeAngelis, Barbara, Ph.D. 1994. *Real Moments.* New York: Bantam Doubleday Dell Publishing Group, Inc.
2. Fryba, Mirko. 1987. *The Practice of Happiness.* Boston: Shambhala Publications, Inc.
3. Jordan, Michael. 1998. *For the Love of the Game.* New York: Crown Publishers, Inc.
4. Kabat-Zinn, Jon. 1994. *Wherever You Go There You Are.* New York: Hyperion.
5. Kaufman, Barry Neil. 1991. *Happiness is a Choice.* New York: Ballantine Books.
6. Mitchell, Steven. 1988. *Tao Te Ching, A New English Version.* New York: Harper & Row, Publishers, Inc.
7. Nhat Hanh, Thich. 1976. *The Miracle of Mindfulness.* Boston: Beacon Press.
8. Nyanaponika Thera. 1972. *The Power of Mindfulness.* San Francisco: Unity Press.
9. Sinetar, Marsha. 1994. *Mindfulness and Meaningful Work.* Berkeley: Parallax Press.
10. Tulku, Tarthang. 1978. *Skillful Means.* Berkeley: Dharma Publishing.
11. Whitmyer, Claude. 1994. *Mindfulness and Meaningful Work.* Berkeley: Parallax Press.
12. Jackson, Phil. 1995. *Sacred Hoops.* New York: Hyperion.
13. Kabat-Zinn, Jon. 1990. *Full Catastrophe Living.* New York: Delacorte Press.